What people are saying about
Overcoming Life's Challenges

"I have greatly enjoyed working through Steve Baird's *Overcoming Life's Challenges* with my men's small group. We found the book to be insightful and helpful in guiding our examination of the scriptural basis for the trials in our lives. I heartily recommend this book both for personal study and for small group use."

Kelly Walter | Founding Pastor | Rock Brook Church

"I want to personally recommend to you, *Overcoming Life's Challenges*, an engaging and enlightening look at chapter one of the epistle of James. Steve has given real insight and application to a unilateral problem that we all face, how can we overcome the harsh reality of heartache, disappointment, and discouragement? How is joy possible in the midst of our struggles? How can I glorify God in this trial?
I encourage you to take the time and read this book, and I'm confident you will reap the benefits."

Dr. Steve Dighton | Pastor Emeritus | Lenexa Baptist Church

"This tome by Steve Baird does not flow from some personal tragedy and as a consequence have limited application; rather his careful exegesis of James 1:1-12 unlocks timeless principles from which anyone may benefit. What I know of his personal life puts added punctuation to that previous comment. Any study group would greatly benefit from a close perusal of this book."

Stanley V. Udd, ThD | Retired Professor of Biblical Languages

"Sports are a microcosm of life, and the Christian athlete can learn much from the trials that regularly show up because of competition. My friend and college basketball teammate, Steve Baird, has persevered through enough of those challenges to complete this quality 'assignment.' I can't think of anyone who would not benefit from reading this book."

John M. Conway | South Central Minnesota Field Associate
Fellowship of Christian Athletes

1

Participant's Guide
Eight Sessions

OVERCOMING LIFE'S CHALLENGES

"Do I Need to Know This for the Final?"

James 1:1-12

By Steve Baird

OVERCOMING LIFE'S CHALLENGES
Do I Need to Know This for the Final?

Copyright © 2019 by Steven Baird

This edition: ISBN 978-1-7323979-2-7

Library of Congress Control Number: 2018910111

Cover design: Sarah Buchan. www.sarahbuchanphotography.com

Contact Steve Baird at: e710ministries@gmail.com

Printed and bound in the United States of America.

DEDICATION

This book is gratefully and lovingly dedicated to my wife, Lisa.
We have overcome life's challenges for 30 years.
I said, "If you marry me, life will never be boring!"
We could use a little boring!

With great appreciation, I would like to acknowledge the
gracious "pilot" small group for *Overcoming Life's Challenges*.
It was a delight to get together each week, look into God's
Word, go through the *Overcoming Life's Challenges* book,
develop friendships, and share together Life's Challenges.
Whether you played a small or a big role in our group, I want
to express my deep appreciation. You will always have a
place in my heart!

A special thank you to:

Lisa
Mike and Ann
Herold and Karen
LaDonna
Cliff and Donna
Nancy

CONTENTS

HOW TO USE THIS PARTICIPANT'S GUIDE

BEFORE THE SESSIONS – For Your Information

➔ *This is a brief description to assist in organizing your group.*

- ### The Group Size

  Overcoming Life's Challenges: What Do I Need to Know for the Final? Participant's Guide and Video sessions are designed to be used in a group setting such as a Bible study, Sunday school class, or any small group gathering. A small group would not want to be any bigger than ten. If you have a larger group, in order to maximize participation, it is recommended that the group break into smaller groups of 4-6 for individual discussion.

- ### The Materials Needed

  The group will need access to the eight video sessions for *Overcoming Life's Challenges*. Each individual will need to have his or her own Participant's Guide. For each session, the Participant's Guide includes video outline notes, directions for activities, and discussion questions. It also contains instructions for **BETWEEN THE SESSIONS - ON YOUR OWN** to guide the participant to process and apply each session. Participants are encouraged to have a copy of the book: *Overcoming Life's Challenges: What Do I Need to Know for the Final?* Reading the book alongside the video and the Participant's Guide will provide more insights to make the experience deeper and richer.

• Group Meeting

It is recommended that the group meet for eight to ten weeks at the same time, day, and location each week. Though the study consists of eight sessions, plan for ten weeks. This will allow you to cancel a week for holidays, weather, illness, etc. It will also allow you to plan for a couple weeks off and/or avail your group of the suggestion items (see facilitator's tips). Each session is designed for ninety minutes, but may be adjusted as needed or wanted. The actual length for each session's video is indicated (for example, 15 minutes) and each of the session's components is given a suggested time (for example, 25 minutes). Also, included with each component is a breakdown of time, for example [25/40]. The first number indicates the length of time devoted to that component, and the second number indicates how far into the session it should take you. Following this format will enable you to complete each session in one and a half hours. Feel free to tailor the study for the needs of your group by allowing more time for one component or eliminating a component.

• The Participant's Guide

This Participant's Guide is purposefully written with a lot of detail. It gives instruction for each component and time allotment. The reason for this is to assist a new or inexperienced Facilitator to have the resources to lead the group. A more seasoned Facilitator will want to adjust the components to tailor his or her group and experience.

- ## Facilitator

Each group will need to appoint a facilitator who is responsible for starting the video and keeping the group on task. Facilitators will want to read the questions aloud, direct the discussions, encourage participants to respond, and assure everyone has the opportunity to participate. See the end of the Participant's Guide for more information and tips for the Facilitator.

DURING THE SESSIONS – With Your Group

→ *This is a brief description of each component of the group meeting.*

- ## Come Together

This is time set aside to build community in your group. These activities are designed to assist you in getting to know and getting closer to other group members.

- ## Watch

Watch the video that corresponds to the session you are studying and discussing.

- ## Group Discussion: What do you think?

Take a few minutes to talk about the video you just watched, discuss the questions, and share your thoughts about the material from the video.

- ## Partner Interaction

  Pair up with 1 or 2 others and work together to discuss or accomplish the activity.

- ## Individual Reflection

  Complete this activity and reflection on your own.

- ## Take Away *My Personal Response*

  ➔ Lord, based on this session, I believe You want me to:

  This is a vital part of each session. Be sure to allow time to complete this statement: *"Lord, based on this session, I believe You want me to..."* The Lord Jesus might want your response to be a change in an attitude, an action, or a decision. Be as specific as you can!

- ## God and I

  This is a time for you, and sometimes others in your group, to spend in prayer. Be real and honest with God about overcoming the challenges you face. Be on the lookout for others who might need prayer and encouragement. Be willing to share your challenges, ask other group members to pray for you, and keep you accountable.

- ## Snacks

  Food always is a good way to help individuals feel more comfortable together and to build relationships. Each week have different individuals from the group volunteer to bring snacks. Also, included is a *"Food for Thot"* fun fact for you to "chew on."

BETWEEN THE SESSIONS – On Your Own

→ This is a critical element to maximize the impact of the study in your personal life. Setting aside time between group sessions for personal study, reflection, and prayer will provide opportunity for life change to take place, which is our goal. Set aside time each week to complete the *Between the Sessions – On Your Own* section. You may want to complete it at one setting or spread it out over a few days. Find what works for your schedule and be faithfully committed to this vital section. *Between the Sessions - On Your Own* consists of three parts:

- **Looking Backward** is a section to direct your thoughts to reflect back on the previous group session and to read the corresponding chapter from book *Overcoming Life's Challenges: What Do I Need to Know for the Final?* (sold separately).

- **Looking Inward** is a section to assist you in processing the session, a closer look at the Scriptures, and the opportunity for applying the session in your personal life.

- **Looking Forward** is a section to begin to focus your thoughts and create interest for the next session.

SESSION 1:
NEXT EXIT: THE SCHOOL OF HARD KNOCKS

Come Together: *"Who's My Neighbor?"*

(30 minutes)   [30/30]

Break the group into pairs. Give each pair about 10 minutes. Instruct them to get to know each other so they can introduce the other one to the larger group with a 1-2 minute introduction. Bring everyone back to the large group and allow for introductions.

Watch: *"Next Exit: The School of Hard Knocks"*

(20 minutes)   [20/50]

Why is the book subtitled: *"Do I Need to Know This for the Final?"*

> "Of course, this question often means: I don't want to study or learn anything I don't absolutely need in order to pass the final test. In life, we tend to be the same way. We want to skate by with minimum effort in overcoming life's challenges. God, however, is not just interested in our "passing" or "failing". He is committed to developing our faith in a way that it will demonstrate itself in the midst of the most trying of tests. God is actively teaching us what He wants us to learn in order to reflect Jesus' character in every area of our lives. Passing or failing this test does not achieve salvation or favor with God; instead it demonstrates and develops the faith we have in Jesus Christ."
>
> *-Overcoming Life's Challenges*

The odds that you and I will experience tests in life are 1 in 1:

→That's _____[1]%!!←

Meet the Teacher Night: The Holy Spirit is our _____[2]!

1. The Holy Spirit is our Divine Teacher.

   But the Advocate, **the Holy Spirit**, whom the Father will send in my name, **will teach you** all things and **will remind** you of everything I have said to you (John 14:26).

   But when he, **the Spirit of truth**, comes, he **will guide you** into all the truth. He will not speak on his own; he will speak only what he hears, and he will tell you what is yet to come (John 16:13).

2. James is our human teacher.

   James, a servant of God and of the Lord Jesus Christ, To the twelve tribes scattered among the nations: Greetings (James 1:1).

"If you do not understand a book by a departed writer you are unable to ask him his meaning,

but the _____[3], who inspired Holy Scripture, lives

forever, and He _____[4] to open the Word to

those who _____[5] His instruction."

-Charles H. Spurgeon, The Prince of Preachers

Preview Day: Jesus is our _____ 6!

1. Jesus motivates us by His **prompting**.

    Being confident of this, that he who began a good work in you will carry it on to completion until the day of Christ Jesus (Philippians 1:6).

> "God _____ 7 us too much to take anything less than an aggressive role in the development of our character."
>
> -Gary Mayes, *Now What*

2. Jesus motivates us by His **presence**.
    Joshua 1:9; Isaiah 43:1-3a; Hebrews 13:4

3. Jesus motivates us by His **power**.
    You, dear children, are from God and have overcome them, because the one who is in you is greater than the one who is in the world (1 John 4:4).

Curriculum Night: God is our _____ 8!

1. God changes us into **demonstrators** of our faith.

    But someone will say, 'You have faith; I have deeds.' Show me your faith without deeds, and **I will show you my faith by my deeds** (James 2:18).

2. God changes us into **doers** of the Word.
    Do not merely listen to the word, and so deceive yourselves. _____9 **what it says** (James 1:22).

"The Christian life is not _____ 10;

it is a _____ 11."

Group Discussion: *"What Do You Think?"*

(10 minutes)   [10/60]

- *"But the Advocate, the Holy Spirit, whom the Father will send in my name, will teach you all things and will remind you of everything I have said to you"* (John 14:26). What are your thoughts about the Holy Spirit being our Teacher?

- Philippians 1:6 tells us, *"being confident of this, that he who began a good work in you will carry it on to completion until the day of Christ Jesus."* How can this tremendous verse be a "theme verse" for us as we attend the School of Hard Knocks and face life's challenges?

Individual Reflection: *"Read James 1:1-12"*

(10 minutes)   [10/70]

Read James 1:1-12 slowly and thoughtfully and answer the following two questions. If you do not get through all the verses in the next 10 minutes or so, you can come back to them this week during your *Between the Sessions - On Your Own* time.

➔ What do I **LEARN** about **TRIALS** from James 1:1-12?

-

-

-

-

-

-

➔ What **QUESTIONS** do I have about **TRIALS** from James 1:1-12?

-

-

-

-

-

Take Away: *"My Personal Response"*

(5 minutes)   [5/75]

➔ Lord, based on this session, I believe You want me to:

God and I:

(5 minutes)   [5/80]

Spend the next few minutes in silent prayer. Thank Jesus for the good work He is continually doing in your life, even when you can't see it or understand it. Pray that you would allow the Holy Spirit to be your Teacher to guide you to truth as you embark on the journey of passing the test of trials.

Snacks:

(10 minutes)   [10/90]

Food for Thot:[A] Ketchup was used as medicine in the 1830s. Maybe that's why my Dad use to squirt ketchup in a teaspoon and eat it. Yuck!

Answers to Video Session 1: 1-100; 2-Teacher; 3-Spirit; 4-Delights; 5-Seek; 6-Motivator; 7-Loves; 8-Transformer; 9-Do; 10-Perfection; 11-Direction

---

[A]All *Food for Thot* comments from: https://spoonuniversity.com/lifestyle/food-facts-you-will-enjoy-reading [accessed 4/9/2018]

BETWEEN THE SESSIONS – ON YOUR OWN
NEXT EXIT: THE SCHOOL OF HARD KNOCKS

LOOKING BACKWARD

- What do you want to remember from video Session 1: *"Next Exit: The School of Hard Knocks"*?

- Read the Introduction, *"Next Exit: The School of Hard Knocks"* in the book *Overcoming Life's Challenges: What Do I Need to Know for the Final?* Note any insights you want to remember from the book. What questions come to mind that you want to think about some more or bring to the group?

Then he said to them all: "Whoever wants to be my disciple must deny themselves and take up their cross daily and follow me. For whoever wants to save their life will lose it, but whoever loses their life for me will save it. What good is it for someone to gain the whole world, and yet lose or forfeit their very self?"

-Jesus (Luke 9:23-25)

LOOKING INWARD

Summary of Session 1: While attending the School of Hard Knocks, 100% of us will experience the test of trials! We can find comfort and strength in the fact that the Holy Spirit is our Teacher, Jesus is doing a good work in us, and God has a purpose in the challenges of life.

"As we embark on his course *"Overcoming Life's Challenges"*, James' own words give us God's desired outcome: *"Do not merely listen to the word, and so deceive yourselves. Do what it says"* (James 1:22). We have to carefully listen to and examine the Word of God, but if we stop at mere knowledge we mislead ourselves into thinking we will pass the tests of trials. This is like memorizing the answers to the final in order to pass but not learning the material to the point that it makes a difference in one's life. James emphatically shouts, **"Do what it says!"** In allowing each of these principles to shape us, the result will be a transformed life. This is the difference the testing of our faith is intended to make in each of us."

-Overcoming Life's Challenges

Challenge-O-Meter:

Luke tells us that while Jesus was here on earth, He grew in four areas: *"And Jesus grew in **wisdom [mentally]** and **stature [physically]**, and in favor with **God [spiritually]** and **man [relationally]**"* (Luke 2:52). These are areas where we face life's challenges. Identify what type of challenge you are facing right now: mental, physical, spiritual, relational or emotional? Give it a description or name. Then on a scale of 1-10 (10 being for the hardest challenge/trial; 1 for the easiest), rate the challenges.

TYPE OF CHALLENGE	DESCRIPTION OR NAME	RATING
Mental		
Physical		
Spiritual		
Relational		
Emotional		
Other		

➜ Which challenge or combination of challenges are the hardest for you right now?

Match Game:

Match the principle with the passage that best reflects God's promise during our trials.

_____ The Holy Spirit promises to be my teacher.

_____ Jesus promises to do a good work in me.

_____ God promises to go with me through the trial.

_____ God promises to have a purpose in my trial.

A. James 1:2-4

B. Isaiah 43:1-3a

C. Philippians 1:6

D. John 14:26

➜ Which of these passages of promise best gives you hope in the midst of your current challenges? Explain.

"Before we can pray, 'Lord, Thy Kingdom come,' we must be willing to pray, 'My Kingdom go.'"

-Alan Redpath

The Observation Tower:

"Being confident of this, that he who began a good work in you will carry it on to completion until the day of Christ Jesus."

Philippians 1:6

"God loves us too much to take anything less than an aggressive role in the development of our character."

-Gary Mayes, *Now What!*

→ When you look at Gary Mayes' quote along with Philippians 1:6, what are three observations you can make about God's work in your life?

1.

2.

3.

On Trial:

God allows and brings trials in our lives for us to demonstrate and develop our faith.

> **"If you were put on trial for being a Christian, would there be enough evidence for a jury to convict you?"**

As you examine the challenges you identified on the **Challenge-O-Meter**, what evidence could be brought against you to say you **were** a Christian?

What evidence could be brought against you to say you **are not** a Christian?

From your answer in the **Match Game** section, what promise of hope does God want you to focus on this week as you face your test of trials?

LOOKING FORWARD

My Teacher Doesn't Like Me!

Have you ever had computer trouble? That's like asking if the sky is blue! I would venture to say that at one time or another we all have had computer trouble, and sometimes we have responded in ways that would have kept us from being convicted as a Christian! When I go to my computer friends for help, they have a few questions, and then ask: "Is your computer plugged in?" "Is it turned on?" I give the answer like, "Duh, the sky is blue, the grass is green, and my computer is...uh...not plugged in!" How foolish we feel, yet that's what it is like so often in our walk with Jesus. In Christ we have the power that raised Him from the dead (Ephesians 1:18-20; 3:14-21), and yet we struggle with the test of trials. Are we plugged into Christ's power, or have we become disconnected? We might give the answer, "Duh, I'm a Christian, I have the resurrection power of Christ available to me...uh...my life is not connected right now." As we move to our next session, be mindful of the words of John, *"You, dear children, are from God and have overcome them, because the one who is in you is greater than the one who is in the world"* (1 John 4:4).

SESSION 2
MY TEACHER DOESN'T LIKE ME!

Yield our Trials to God's Power - James 1:1

Come Together: *"Highs and Lows"*

(20 minutes)   [20/20]

Ask each person to think of his or her High Point and Low Point over the last month. Depending on the size of your group, go around the circle and have everyone share. If needed, your group can break into 2 or 3 smaller groups. This will allow for each to share during the allotted time.

Watch: *"My Teacher Doesn't Like Me!"*

(15 minutes)   [15/35]

"When encountering the testing of our faith, we may feel Jesus is distant, uncaring, or doesn't even like us. As the test unfolds, we may now know or understand what God is teaching us. It is difficult to trust Him. Like the teacher, He knows the material completely and the best way for each of us to learn the eternal lessons. In the end, we realize God cares more about our spiritual maturity than our earthly comfort. He is passionate and actively involved in preparing us to live a life that reflects Jesus Christ."

-Overcoming Life's Challenges

31

WE PASS THE TEST OF TRIALS

BY YIELDING OUR TRIALS TO **GOD'S POWER**.

→ God's Power raised Jesus from the dead (Ephesians 1:19-20). That's power! To unleash God's Power does not mean we control God or His Power but as we yield ourselves to Him we become a conduit for God's Power to live through us.

God's Power is Unleashed through us by Surrendering our _____[1].

"James, a servant of God"
James 1:1a

→ When I surrender my will I am saying:

1. "I am God's slave." James = slave [*doulos*]

   Exodus 21:2-6b, "Then he will be his servant for life"

2. "I am making a _____[2] commitment to serve Jesus Christ."[B]
   1 Corinthians 6:19-20

"If we understand that everything happening to us is to make us more Christ-like, it will solve a great deal of anxiety in our lives."

-A.W. Tozer, *The Crucified Life*

[B] I want to express my appreciation for insights from Pastor Ryland Walter's sermon, "The Heart of a Servant," preached at Rock Brook Church, September 2-3, 2017.

God's Power is Unleashed through us by Relinquishing our _____.[3]

"James, a servant of God and the Lord Jesus Christ"
James 1:1a

➔ When I let go of my control I am saying:

1. "I am a control freak."

2. "I acknowledge Jesus Christ is Lord."
   (cm. Philippians 2:9-11)

3. "I accept the fact that God does as He pleases."

   Our God is in heaven; he does whatever **pleases** him (Psalm 115:3).

   The Lord does whatever **pleases** him, in the heavens and on the earth, in the seas and all their depths (Psalm 135:6).

   The Sovereignty of God is like petting a _____.[4]

God's Power is Unleashed through us by Reaching Out to _____.[5]

"To the twelve tribes scatted among the nations: Greetings."
James 1:1b

Praise be to the God and Father of our Lord Jesus Christ, the Father of Compassion and the God of all comfort, who comforts us in all our troubles, so that we can comfort those in any trouble with the comfort we ourselves have received from God (2 Corinthians 1:3-4).

"Jesus is _____[6] in the _____[7]!"

Snacks:

(15 minutes)   [15/50]

Food for Thot: In the state of Kentucky, it is illegal to hold an ice cream cone in your back pocket. If you choose to break the law and you're on the run, whatever you do, do not stop and sit down! .

Group Discussion: *"What Do You Think?"*

(25 minutes)   [25/75]

→ Feel free to grab some more snacks and a drink and gather around to watch the Video.

- Share your thoughts about the story of Thomas Haukes. How does Haukes' life demonstrate the principles of this session?

> **"The mark of a saint is not perfection, but consecration. A saint is not a man without faults, but a man who has given himself without reserve to God."**
>
> -Brooke Foss Westcott

- Typically, what comes to mind when you think about being a servant/slave of God? **"I am making a lifetime commitment to serve Jesus Christ."** How does this statement change your understanding of what it means to be a "slave of God?

- Come on admit it: "Hi, I'm _____ and I'm a "control freak" when it comes to _____?

- **Jesus is the Sovereign Controller and does as He pleases.** What comforts you about that statement? What makes the hair on the back of your neck stand up when it comes to this statement? Why might you experience both ends of the spectrum regarding this statement?

- Share a time when you experienced a trial and then were able to help someone else because of that trial.

> **"God does not comfort us to make us comfortable but to make us comforters."**
>
> -John Jowett

Take Away: *"My Personal Response"*

(5 minutes) [5/80]

→ Lord, based on this session, I believe You want me to:

God and I:

(10 minutes) [10/90]

Gather in a group of 2 or 3. Briefly, have each share a prayer request and then pray for each other.

Answers to Video Session 2: 1-Will; 2-Lifetime; 3-Control; 4-Cat; 5-Others; 6-LORD; 7-Fire

BETWEEN THE SESSIONS - ON YOUR OWN

My Teacher Doesn't Like Me!

Yield Our Trials to God's Power - James 1:1

LOOKING BACKWARD

- What do you want to remember from video Session 2: *"My Teacher Doesn't Like Me!"*?

- Read Chapter 1: *"My Teacher Doesn't Like Me!"* in the book *Overcoming Life's Trials: What Do I Need to Know for the Final?* Note any insights you want to remember from the book. What questions come to mind that you want to think about some more or bring to the group?

LOOKING INWARD

Summary of Session 2: As we give the steering wheel of our lives to Jesus Christ, the same resurrection power enables us to overcome life's challenges. James in his usual "in your face" style, addresses three issues in yielding our trials to God's Power. When we become a slave we are saying, "I am making a lifetime commitment to serve Jesus Christ." When we are calling Jesus Lord we are saying, "Jesus you can do as you please in my life." Through the hurts, the confusion, and the trials Jesus wants us to reach out to others.

"We long for that day when all those pagans, derelicts, degenerates, jerks, idiots, spouses, bosses, neighbors, athletes, actors, musicians, politicians will *'at the name of Jesus bow their knee'* and *'their tongues declare that Jesus Christ is Lord to the glory of God the Father'* (see Philippians 2:9-11). There is one person we don't include in that list, that one person looks back at us in the mirror. We struggle with bowing the knee of our heart before the Lord Jesus and using our tongue to declare Jesus as Lord, because when we do, we are clearly saying we are not in control."

-Overcoming Life's Challenges

Self-Evaluation:

For each of the following statements, check the box that best describes you or make your own statement.

➜ Right now, when it comes to being a **slave to God... MASTER**

☐ I am bothered and/or confused about the biblical idea of a slave.

☐ I am a servant that gets the orders and goes and does it on my own.

☐ I have made a lifetime commitment to serve Jesus Christ.

☐ Other:

> **"If you live for people's acceptance, you'll die from their rejection."**
>
> -Lecrae, Musician

➔ Right now, when it comes to making **Jesus Lord...CONTROLLER**

- ☐ I feel like it is selfish of Jesus to do as He pleases.
- ☐ I like the fact that Jesus is in control and all powerful when it suits me.
- ☐ I am content to allow Jesus to be Lord of my life, including challenges.
- ☐ Other:

➔ Right now, when it comes to reaching out **to others...COMFORTER**

- ☐ I have a hard time looking past my own issues and concerns.
- ☐ I like to help but feel like I've been hurt so I'm guarded.
- ☐ I look for opportunities to use my trials to help and comfort others.
- ☐ Other:

> **"It is doubtful whether God can bless a man greatly until He has hurt him deeply."**
>
> -A.W. Tozer

Face Your Challenge:

→ This is how I would describe the challenge I am facing this week:

→ To face your challenge this week, pick one of the following principles and passages you believe God wants you to focus on. Drawing insight from the one you chose; write two very simple, realistic, and practical steps you can take to attack your challenge.

☐ **Jesus is my Master: I will serve Him.**
Do you not know that your bodies are temples of the Holy Spirit, who is in you, whom you have received from God? You are not your own; you were bought at a price. Therefore honor God with your bodies (1 Corinthians 6:19-20).

➢

➢

> "I have put my soul, as a blank [check], into the hands of Jesus Christ my Redeemer, and desired Him to write upon it what He pleases. I know it will be His own image."
>
> -George Whitefield

☐ Jesus is my Controller: I will surrender to Him.

The LORD does whatever pleases him, in the heavens and on the earth, in the seas and all their depths (Psalm 135:6).

➢

➢

☐ Jesus is my Comforter: I will comfort others.

Praise be to the God and Father of our Lord Jesus Christ, the Father of compassion and the God of all comfort, ⁴ who comforts us in all our troubles, so that we can comfort those in any trouble with the comfort we ourselves receive from God (2 Corinthians 1:3-4).

➢

➢

My Own Words:

Jesus as our Master and Jesus as our Controller are two of the foundational blocks we build to overcome life's challenges. Now that we've looked at them from several different angles, take a step back, and gaze at the whole building. If someone would ask you what these characteristics of Jesus mean in the storms of life, how would you describe each one? (Sorry to make you think...not really!)

→ **Jesus as our Master**

→ **Jesus as our Controller**

Jesus Lord In My Fire:

Jesus may not ask you to be burnt at the stake or to die for Him like Thomas Haukes, but He is asking you to live for Him. How does Thomas Haukes' story encourage you to endure the fiery trial you are experiencing right now

---

Dear friends, do not be surprised at the fiery ordeal that has come on you to test you, as though something strange were happening to you.

1 Peter 4:12

LOOKING FORWARD

But I Experience Test Anxiety!

"I can't see the forest for the trees" is an often used cliché; however, at times it is a fitting description of our lives. Our challenges and trials so consume our thoughts, emotions, and daily living that we cannot step back and see what God is doing. His viewpoint or perspective is critical to our "I-sight". We are encouraged to put on His lens to see our challenges as He sees them and to allow Jesus to make the necessary adjustments to bring those trials into focus. As we take the next step of our journey with Jesus consider Paul's words of perspective: *"Since, then, you have been raised with Christ, set your hearts on things above, where Christ is, seated at the right hand of God. Set your minds on things above, not on earthly things. For you died, and your life is now hidden with Christ in God"* (Colossians 3:1-3).

SESSION 3

BUT I EXPERIENCE TEST ANXIETY!

See Our Trials from God's Perspective

- James 1:2

Snacks:

(20 minutes) [20/20]

Food for Thot: Arachibutyrophobia is the fear of getting peanut butter stuck to the top of your mouth. Yes, this is a real fear, but I can't talk about it because something is stuck to the roof of my mouth!

→ Feel free to grab some more snacks and a drink and gather around to watch the Video.

Watch: *"But I Experience Test Anxiety!"*

(20 minutes) [20/40]

"A simple definition is 'a trial is a test.' It is a test to find out the character of someone."

-Overcoming Life's Challenges

WE PASS THE TEST OF TRIALS
BY SEEING OUR TRIALS FROM
GOD'S PERSPECTIVE.

God's Perspective Gives Us _____[1] in Our Trials. James 1:2a

Consider it pure joy, my brothers and sisters,...
James 1:2a

1. To have joy in our trials, it is important how we look at trials.

   > **Consider =**
   > *"in my mind's eye"*

   ➤ **God's Perspective is seeing life the way He sees it and living life from God's _____.[2]**

2. To have full joy in our trials, it is important we look to the Lord for strength.

   Do not grieve, **for the joy of the Lord is your strength** (Nehemiah 8:10b; also see Nehemiah 12:43).

"Not by might nor by power, but by my Spirit,"
says the Lord Almighty.

Zechariah 4:6b

God's Perspective Gives Us _____ [3] of Our Trials. James 1:2b

Consider it pure joy, my brothers and sisters, whenever you face trials of many kinds,...
James 1:2

1. The Definition of Trials:

   ➢ A simple definition is: "A trial is a _____."[4]

   ➢ James gives us this definition for trials.

   "A trial is a test that God uses to _____[5] the genuineness of our faith and to _____[6] our maturity in Jesus Christ."

2. The Lens of Adjustment:

   Adjustment #1: Trials will happen!
   "...whenever..." James 1:2

   Adjustment #2: Trials will meet us in the natural pathways of our lives!
   "...you face..." James 1:2

   Adjustment #3: Trials will come in many sizes, shapes, shades, and degrees!
   "...many kinds..." James 1:2

   Adjustment #4: Trials will test our faith!
   "...because you know that the testing of your faith develops perseverance." James 1:3

"One Degree Off Course"

Come Together: *"The Eye Clinic"*

(15 minutes) [10/50]

As you think about the challenges in your life this week, what kind of glasses would you put on? Explain your answer.

- ❏ Sunglasses
- ❏ Reading glasses
- ❏ Driving glasses
- ❏ Magnifying glasses
- ❏ Glasses with no lens
- ❏ Protective glasses
- ❏ Other:

Group Discussion: *"What Do You Think?"*

(25 minutes) [25/75]

- • What is God's perspective? How does the illustration of the tinted sunglasses help your understanding of seeing life, especially trials, from God's perspective?

- Discuss our definition of a trial: *"A trial is a test God uses to prove the genuineness of our faith and to develop our maturity in Jesus Christ."* What part of the definition helps you understand trials? What questions do you have about James' definition of trials?

- Why do you think the example *"One Degree Off Course"* is so important to understanding God's Perspective? What are some thoughts, attitudes, actions, or influences that can cause us get one degree off God's course? What can we do get back on God's course?

> **"The only thing you sometimes have control over is perspective. You don't have control over your situation. But you have a choice about how you view it."**
>
> -Chris Pine

Take Away: *"My Personal Response"*

(5 minutes)   [5/80]

→ Lord, based on this session, I believe You want me to:

God and I:

(10 minutes)   [10/90]

Gather together. Take one prayer request. Then have someone pray for that request. After that prayer take one more prayer request and immediately have someone pray for that request. Continue this process as long as you have time. You are encouraged to write those requests below and pray for them until your next meeting.

Answers to Video Session 3: 1-Joy; 2-Viewopoint; 3-Acceptance; 4-Test; 5-Prove; 6-Develop

BETWEEN THE SESSIONS – ON YOUR OWN
But I Experience Test Anxiety!
See Our Trials from God's Perspective
-James 1:2

LOOKING BACKWARD

- What do you want to remember from video Session 3: *"But I Experience Test Anxiety!"*?

- Read Chapter 2: *"But I experience Test Anxiety!"* in the book *Overcoming Life's Challenges: Do I Need to Know This for the Final?* Note any insights you want to remember from the book. What questions come to mind that you want to think about some more or bring to the group?

LOOKING INWARD

Summary of Session 3: It is difficult to have God's Perspective in the challenges of life. In James 1:2, we find two very practical ways to gain God's Perspective in the midst of our trials. First, seeing our trials from God's Perspective gives us joy in our trials. Second, seeing our trials from God's Perspective gives us acceptance of our trials.

"As James begins to unveil the painting entitled *Trials*, he reveals something of vital importance; God's perspective. Because of sin, we are wired to look at the tests of life through an earthly, bottom-up lens, and can easily miss viewing our trials through a godly, top-down lens. Having **God's perspective is seeing life the way He sees it and living life from that viewpoint.** This is also known as wisdom."

-Overcoming Life's Challenges

Testophobia:[c]

Do you have testophobia? Tests may not bring much anxiety to you. With the exception of One, we all have fears that can be described as being a bit irrational. Face your fears by identifying the following phobia with its corresponding description. (Answers at end of session.)

____ Ablutophobia

____ Coulrophobia

____ Ephebiphobia

____ Nomophobia

____ Porphyrophobia

____ Panphobia (Omniphobia)

A. The fear of clowns

B. The fear of cleaning oneself

C. The fear of the color purple

D. The fear of everything

E. The fear of teenagers

F. The fear of no mobile phone coverage

[c]https://www.verywellmind.com/most-common-phobias-4136563 [accessed 5/8/2018]

Joy or Acceptance:

When we look at our trials from God's Perspective, we discovered two principles: 1) God's Perspective gives us **joy** in our trials; 2) God's Perspective gives us **acceptance** of our trials. Read the following verses. Decide which passages speaks of God's Perspective of joy and which speak of God's Perspective of acceptance in our challenges. In a few of the verses you may identify both principles. Put the appropriate letter in the blank to identify

> **"God has to take our eyes off our kingdom before He can build His."**
>
> -J.D. Greear
> *Gaining by Losing*

what aspect of the principle of God's Perspective that passage is discussing.

J=Joy   A=Acceptance   B=Both

_____ **Job 14:1 (NET);** Man, born of woman, lives but a few days, and they are full of trouble.

_____ **Nehemiah 8:10;** Nehemiah said, "Go and enjoy choice food and sweet drinks, and send some to those who have nothing prepared. This day is holy to our Lord. Do not grieve, for the joy of the Lord is your strength."

_____ **Proverbs 3:4-5;** Trust in the LORD with all your heart and lean not on your own understanding; in all your ways submit to him, and he will make your paths straight.

_____ **John 16:33;** I have told you these things, so that in me you may have peace. In this world you will have trouble. But take heart! I have overcome the world.

_____ **Hebrews 12:1-2;** Therefore, since we are surrounded by such a great cloud of witnesses, let us throw off everything that hinders and the sin that so easily entangles. And let us run with perseverance the race marked out for us, fixing our eyes on Jesus, the pioneer and perfecter of faith. For the joy set before him he endured the cross, scorning its shame, and sat down at the right hand of the throne of God.

_____ **1 Peter 1:6-7;** In all this you greatly rejoice, though now for a little while you may have had to suffer grief in all kinds of trials. These have come so that the proven genuineness of your faith—of greater worth than gold, which perishes even though refined by fire—may result in praise, glory and honor when Jesus Christ is revealed.

_____ **1 Peter 4:12-13;** Dear friends, do not be surprised at the fiery ordeal that has come on you to test you, as though something strange were happening to you. But rejoice inasmuch as you participate in the sufferings of Christ, so that you may be overjoyed when his glory is revealed.

→ Identify which of these passages best gives you **God's Perspective of joy in trials**. From this verse what would you tell a friend who is struggling with God's Perspective of joy in the challenges of life?

→ Identify which of these passages best gives you **God's Perspective of acceptance in trials.** From this verse what would you tell a friend who is struggling with God's Perspective of acceptance in the challenges of life?

Think About This:

The definition of trials that James gives us is: *A trial is a test God uses to prove the genuineness of our faith and to develop our maturity in Jesus Christ.* In this session we focused on the first part *"A trial is a test God uses...."* In our next session we will focus on the rest of the definition.

→ Think about the trials and challenges you face. How would you compare your trials to a test?

→ Think about the trials and challenges you face. How is God using the trials in your life?

MY ONE DEGREE:

Fill in the chart below. Spend time talking with the Heavenly Father about the challenges you are facing, what His perspective is for you, and what is causing you to veer off His course for you.

	CHALLENGES I AM FACING	GOD'S PERSPECTIVE OF MY CHALLENGES	THIS IS GETTING ME OFF COURSE
1			
2			
3			

LOOKING FORWARD

When Will I Ever Use This In Real Life?

As we proceed on the journey to our next session, the writer to the Hebrews creates a spectacular bridge from **God's Perspective** to **God's Purpose** in trials. *"Therefore, since we are surrounded by such a huge crowd of witnesses to the life of faith, let us strip off every weight that slows us down, especially the sin that so easily trips us up. And let us run with endurance the race God has set before us. We do this by keeping our eyes on Jesus, the champion who initiates and perfects our faith. Because of the joy awaiting him, he endured the cross, disregarding its shame. Now he is seated in the place of honor beside God's throne"* (Hebrews 12:1-2 NLT). Joy motivated Jesus to endure the cross because He saw the work of the cross from God's Perspective. God's Perspective also enabled Jesus to understand God's Purpose in the cross. The cross gave Jesus a place of honor and provided us with salvation through His name. Now that we have examined **God's Perspective**, let's look closely at **God's Purpose** for us in our trials.

Testophobia Answers:

- ✓ **Ablutophobia** - the fear of cleaning oneself
- ✓ **Coulrophobia** - the fear of clowns
- ✓ **Ephebiphobia** - the fear of teenagers
- ✓ **Nomophobia** - the fear of no mobile phone coverage
- ✓ **Porphyrophobia** - the fear of the color purple
- ✓ **Panphobia (or Omniphobia)** - the fear of everything

SESSION 4

WHEN WILL I EVER USE THIS IN REAL LIFE?

Understand Our Trials accomplish

God's Purpose - James 1:3-4

Come Together: *"What's The Purpose of This Object?"*

**Also, collect prayer requests, names, and emails.*

(25 minutes)   [25/25]

- **Before the group arrives:** On a table or flat surface place 4-5 objects and cover each item separately with a towel or blanket. [Facilitators, for a twist on this *Come Together Activity* check *Come Together Activities* session #4 in the back of this guide.]

- **As group members arrive:** On a 3x5 card, ask each person to put his/her name, email, and a prayer request.

- **As the meeting starts:** Ask for 2 volunteers. Explain: as they go down the line of covered items, they will pick up the towel/blanket, identify the object, and state what its purpose is. Select one volunteer to go 1st and ask the other one to go to another room. After the 1st volunteer finishes ask the 2nd volunteer to come in for his/her turn. Let them know that they will be timed. The individual with the fastest time to correctly identify the object and its purpose will determine the winner. Facilitator, make sure you have a prize for the winner!!

Watch: *"When Will I Ever Use This in Real Life?"*
(20 minutes)   [20/45]

"How many times does God use the test of trials in our lives to bring about His desired life change, yet we get sidetracked by asking questions like: 'When will I ever use this in real life?' 'What does this have to do with my life?' 'Why is God allowing this trial in my life?' When we say this, we have neither fully grasped nor fully accepted God's purpose in trials. Whether we recognize it or not, the tests of trials, more than academics, prepare us for life both now and in eternity."

-Overcoming Life's Challenges

WE PASS THE TEST OF TRIALS BY UNDERSTANDING OUR TRIALS ACCOMPLISH GOD'S PURPOSE.

God's Purpose in Trials is to Demonstrate Our Faith is _____[1]. James 1:3

Because you know that the testing of your faith develops perseverance...
James 1:3

> **Know** means "to know by experience" or "to allow someone to participate in life with us."

> **Testing** means "approved after testing, tested and approved, the genuine part."[D]

For example: the 1972 Miami Dolphins' Football

> **Perseverance** means to remain under. "The picture is of a person successfully carrying a heavy load for a long time."[E]

Let us not lose heart in doing good, for in due time we will reap if we do not grow weary (Galatians 6:9 NASB).

[D]Fritz Rienecker and Cleon L. Rogers, Jr., A Linguistic Key to the Greek New Testament (Grand Rapids, MI: The Zondervan Corporation, Regency Reference Library, 1980), 721.

[E]Douglas J. Moo, The Letter of James: The Pillar New Testament Commentary (Grand Rapids: Eerdmans, 2000), 6.

God's Purpose in Trials is to Develop Our Faith into the _____[2] of Christ. James 1:4

**Perseverance must finish its work so that you may be mature and complete not lacking anything.
James 1:4**

> **Finish** means to accomplish or finish its work.
> [cm. John 19:30, "It is finished."]

> **Mature** means to bring to maturity and **Complete** means complete in all its parts, an entirety.

Keep your

_____ [3]

On

_____ **!**[4]

Therefore, since we are surrounded by such a great cloud of witnesses, let us throw off everything that hinders and the sin that so easily entangles. And let us run with perseverance the race marked out for us, fixing our eyes on Jesus, the pioneer and perfecter of faith. For the joy set before him he endured the cross, scorning its shame, and sat down at the right hand of the throne of God.

Hebrews 12:1-2

Partner Interaction: *"Talk it over with a Friend"*

(10 minutes)   [10/55]

Get with one or two others and discuss the following from the video.

➔ When it comes to the purpose of trials in my life, I found this helpful:

➔ When it comes to the purpose of trials in my life, I wrestle with this:

Group Discussion: *"What Do You Think?"*

(15 minutes)   [15/70]

"A trial is a test God uses to prove the genuineness of our faith and to develop our maturity in Jesus Christ."

➔ Why do you think God uses trials to prove the genuineness of our faith?

➔ How have you observed God using trials to develop your faith?

➔ What comparisons can you draw between the marathon race that John Stephen Akhwari of Tanzania ran and the Christian life we run?

> "Sometimes you face difficulties not because you're doing something wrong, but because you're doing something right."

Take Away: *"My Personal Response"*

(5 minutes)   [5/75]

➔ Lord, based on this session, I believe You want me to:

"And you shall remember the whole way that the LORD your God has led you these forty years in the wilderness, that he might humble you, testing you to know what was in your heart, whether you would keep his commandments or not"

Deuteronomy 8:2 (ESV)

God and I:

(5 minutes) [5/80]

Give one of the 3x5 cards, which were filled out upon arrival, to each group member. No one may take their own card or a spouse's. It is encouraged to give men's cards to men and women's cards to women. Once everyone has received a card, instruct him/her to pray for that person each day between now and the next meeting. Ask each person to email the group member he/she is praying for one time this week. The email should be encouraging and to let that person know they are being uplifted in prayer. Use other methods of communication, if you would like or feel comfortable.

Snacks:

(10 minutes) [10/90]

Food for Thot: Chocolate was once used as a currency. They probably had to change it because people kept eating their assets.

Answers to Video Session 4: 1-Genuine; 2-Maturity; 3-Eyes; 4-Jesus

BETWEEN THE SESSIONS - ON YOUR OWN
When Will I Ever Use This In Real Life?

Understand Our Trials Accomplish

God's Purpose - James 1:3-4

LOOKING BACKWARD

- What do you want to remember from video Session 4: *"When Will I Ever Use This in Real Life?"*

- Read Chapter 3: *"When Will I Ever Use This in Real Life?"* in the book *Overcoming Life's Trials: Do I Need to Know This for the Final?* Note any insights you want to remember from the book. What questions come to mind that you want to think about some more or bring to the group?

LOOKING INWARD

Summary of Session 4: James gives clarity to God's Purpose in facing the challenges of life. Our definition is ***"A trial is a test God uses to prove the genuineness of our faith and to develop our maturity in Jesus Christ."*** Each and every trial we experience has real life implications, and we can pass the test of trials as we understand our trials accomplish God's purpose: 1) to demonstrate our faith is genuine; 2) to develop our maturity in Christ.

"Sometimes, the question of "why" must be replaced with the question of "what." James moves from why God brings trials to what God is doing in trials. Why the testing of our faith? Because God wants us to demonstrate our faith is real. What is God doing in the testing of our faith? He is developing our spiritual maturity to be more and more like Jesus Christ. Honestly, the lantern of "why" does not always give us enough light to see its answer, but the lantern of "what" does gives clarity to see what God is doing."

-Overcoming Life's Challenges

Thought Provokers:

Regarding the Challenges I am facing right now:

➔ How does God want me to demonstrate my faith is genuine?

➔ What is God doing to develop my faith into Christ-likeness?

➔ How do my challenges help me relate to Job?

➔ What would God whisper in my ear?

Dig Deeper:

Reason #1: God's Purpose in trials is to demonstrate our faith is genuine. *"Because you know that the testing of your faith develops perseverance"* (James 1:3). From this verse and principle, what are three observations you can make?

    1.

    2.

    3.

Reason #2: God's Purpose in trials is to develop our faith into the maturity of Christ. *"Perseverance must finish its work so that you may be mature and complete not lacking anything"* (James 1:4). From this verse and principle, what are three observations you can make?

    1.

    2.

    3.

➔From this **Dig Deeper** section, what do you want to remember in the midst of your current challenges? What difference will that make as you face your trials?

Essential Ingredients:

Every baker knows there are essential ingredients used to make a cake, and the ingredients must be added in the correct proportions. Purpose in trials is God's cake. He adds and stirs in His essential ingredients at the right time and in the proper amount. In chapter 1 verses 3 and 4, James uses several words to describe God's Essential Ingredients for purpose in trials. Based on what you've learned: 1) Put each Essential Word Ingredient into your own words; 2) Explain how each of these words are an Essential Ingredient in making the cake of purpose in trials. You may want to refer back to the outline under the Watch the Video section (or chapter 3 – "When Will I Ever Use This in Real Life?" in the book) to assist you and refresh your memory.

- **Know**

- **Testing**

- **Perseverance**

- **Finish**

- **Mature and complete**

However, when ambassadors arrived from Babylon to ask about the remarkable events that had taken place in the land, God withdrew from Hezekiah in order to test him and to see what was really in his heart.

2 Chronicles 32:31 (NLT)

What Is Jesus Doing:

➔ Pick one: What is the trial you are facing right now?

- ☐ Mental
- ☐ Physical
- ☐ Emotional
- ☐ Relational
- ☐ Spiritual
- ☐ Combination

➔ Pick one:

- ☐ God is at work in me to demonstrate my faith is real.
- ☐ God is at work in me to develop my faith into Christ-likeness.

➔ Which essential ingredient do you need to add? How will you do that?

- ☐ Know:
- ☐ Testing:
- ☐ Perseverance:
- ☐ Finish:
- ☐ Mature and Complete:

LOOKING FORWARD

Isn't the Learning Center for Dummies?

In our trials, we can put on God's glasses of perspective and even adjust them to bring His perspective into focus. Our minds can mentally ascend to the fact that God is actively at work in our lives demonstrating the genuineness of our faith and developing our faith into the likeness of Jesus Christ. But as long as we traverse this globe, **we will have tests and we will struggle with them!** So, what do we do? Fortunately, James has not led us up the side of the mountain, only to abandon us as the road gets steeper, the air gets thinner, and the peak gets obscure. James will have us stop; look out over God's ravine to see the beauty of His view, God's incredible character; and will have us ask as the disciples did, *"Lord, teach us to pray"* (Luke 11:1).

"By perseverance, the snail reached the ark."

-Charles Haddon Spurgeon

SESSION 5

ISN'T THE LEARNING CENTER FOR DUMMIES?

Allow Our Trials to teach us God's Prayer

-James 1:5-8

Watch: *"Isn't the Learning Center for Dummies?"*

(20 minutes)   [20/20]

"Here is where prayer comes in to overcome life's challenges. Prayer is not merely for those who need a crutch to lean on in difficulties. Instead we are commanded to pray and ask for wisdom during our trials. Whether we are failing the tests of trials or just want to improve, prayer is one of the key components of aligning ourselves with God's perspective and accomplishing God's purpose during our seasons of trials. It is comparable to a college Learning Center."

-Overcoming Life's Challenges

WE PASS THE TEST OF TRIALS BY ALLOWING OUR TRIALS TO TEACH US GOD'S PRAYER.

God's Prayer Teaches Us To Look At Our Trials From God's_____.[1] James 1:5a

**If any of you lacks wisdom, he should ask God,...
James 1:5a**

1. We pray because **we are deficient**.

   "But if...we are deficient in wisdom..."

2. We pray because **God is sufficient**.

   *"If any of you lacks wisdom, **he should ask God,...**"*

   ➢ We are commanded to ask God, not anybody else. 1:5a

   ➢ We are commanded to ask God with a sense of urgency and longing.

   Let us then approach God's throne of grace with confidence, so that we may receive mercy and find grace to help us in our time of need (Hebrews 4:16).

God's Prayer Teaches Us To Commit Our Trials To God's_____2.

James 1:5b

If any of you lacks wisdom, you should ask
**God, who gives generously to all without finding fault,
and it will be given to you.**
James 1:5b

**The fear of the Lord is the beginning of wisdom, and
knowledge of the Holy One is understanding.
Proverbs 9:10**

The Riches of Our God:

1. God is a **giving** God.
   "God who gives…"

2. God is a **generous** God.
   "…generously…"

3. God is an **impartial** God.
   "…to all…"

4. God is a **gracious** God.
   "…without fault…"

5. God is a **promise-keeping** God.
   "…it will be given to you."

> **Giving =Loving**
>
> For God so **loved** the world that he **gave** his one and only Son
>
> John 3:16a

75

God's Prayer Teaches Us To Entrust Our Trials To God _____.[3] James 1:6-8

"The true end of prayer is to get our wills harmonized with His, _____[4] to bend His to ours."

–Alexander Maclaren, Ministered in Manchester, England

1. Doubters are **disputers**.
   "But when you ask, you must believe and not doubt, because the one who doubts is like a wave of the sea, blown and tossed by the wind" (James 1:6).

2. Doubters are **delusional**.
   "That person should not expect to receive anything from the Lord" (James 1:7).

3. Doubters are **divided**.
   "Such a person is double-minded…" (James 1:8a).

4. Doubters are **disastrous**.
   "…and unstable in all they do" (James 1:8b).

George Müller

"I need not despair because the living God is my partner. I do not have sufficient wisdom to meet these difficulties, but He is able to direct me. I can pour out my heart to God and ask Him to guide and direct me and to supply me with wisdom. Then I have to believe that He will do so. I can go with good courage to my business and expect help from Him in the next difficulty that may come before me."

Snacks:

(15 minutes) [15/35]

Food for Thot: In South Africa, it is common to roast up termites and ants and call them popcorn. A word to the wise!

Group Discussion: *What Do You Think?*

(20 minutes) [20/55]

→ Feel free to grab some more snacks and a drink and gather around to watch the Video.

- What does the illustration of *The Parade* teach us about praying for wisdom (God's Perspective) in Life's Challenges?

- *"The fear of the Lord is the beginning of wisdom, and the knowledge of the Holy One is understanding."* *(Proverbs 9:10)* Why is the connection between knowing God and the prayer for wisdom so important?

- Alexander Maclaren stated, *"The true end of prayer is to get our wills harmonized with His, not to bend His to ours."* What does that statement say to you about the trials of your life?

- When it comes to prayer and the challenges of life, George Müller is a remarkable example for us. Share your thoughts and observations about George Müller's prayer life and challenges.

Take Away: *My Personal Response*

(5 minutes)   [5/60]

**When you seek me in prayer and worship, you will find me available to you.
If you seek me with all your heart and soul.**

Jeremiah 29:13 (NET)

→ Lord, based on this session, I believe You want me to:

> **"A Christian without an active prayer life is the functional equivalent of a practicing Atheist."**
>
> **Unknown**

God and I:

(30 minutes)   [30/90]

We don't want to just talk about prayer, let's spend time in prayer. The Group Facilitator will lead you through the following acronym **P.R.A.Y.**

Praise: **(10 minutes)**

James tells us five characteristics of God in verse 5 (listed below). As a group, use sentence prayers to praise God for who He is.

God, who gives generously to all without finding fault, and it will be given to him. James 1:5

☐ God is a **giving** God. *"God who gives..."*

☐ God is a **generous** God. *"God who gives generously..."*

☐ God is an **impartial** God. *"God who gives generously to all..."*

☐ God is a **gracious** God. *"God who gives generously to all without finding fault..."*

☐ God is a **promise-keeping** God. *"God who gives generously to all without finding fault, and it will be given to him.*

Repent: (5 minutes)

James instructs us to believe and not doubt. Spend a few minutes on your own asking God how you are a doubter and ask him to forgive you. A couple of thoughts below will help guide your prayer.

□ Lord, here is how my doubts are blowing and tossing me like the wind:

□ Lord, here is how my doubts are deceiving me into thinking you will still answer my prayer:

□ Lord, here is how my doubts are keeping me from being wholeheartedly committed to Jesus Christ:

> **"Prayer in the midst of trouble helps us to see God again. It gets our eye off our problems and focuses us afresh on God, who is all-powerful, merciful, and just."**
>
> -Joseph M. Stowell, *The Upside of Down*

Ask: (10 minutes)

Divide into groups of two or three. Use the thoughts below to assist you in asking for wisdom in an area of trial. Pray for yourself and/or the others in your group.

☐ **Ask** God to enable you to see your challenges from His perspective, as though you are in a helicopter looking at a parade.

☐ **Ask** God to bring to mind one of His characteristics or a verse for you to focus on during your test of trials.

☐ **Ask** God to give you a wholehearted commitment to Him and strength to stand against the doubt you just talked with Him about (remember **R**epent above).

Yield: (5 minutes)

Again spend some time alone with God. Use Alexander Maclaren's statement below as a springboard for your prayer time. Pray for the challenge you are facing that you would harmonize your will to God's. Yield yourself to God in order to be in tune with Him.

Never stop praying. 1 Thessalonians 5:17 (NLT)

➔ Before the session closes make two appointments to meet with God this week.

➔ Use the **P.R.A.Y.** model to guide your prayer time.

I will plan on _____ at _____.

                   (Day of week)   (Time of Day)

I will plan on _____ at _____.

                   (Day of week)   (Time of Day)

> **"Get on your knees and fight like a man!"**
>
> -Bob Hartman

Answers to Video Session 5: 1-Viewpoint; 2-Character; 3-Wholeheartedly; 4-Not

BETWEEN THE SESSIONS – ON YOUR OWN
Isn't The Learning Center For Dummies?
Allow Our Trials to teach us God's Prayer

-James 1:5-8

LOOKING BACKWARD

- What do you want to remember from video Session 5: *"Isn't the Learning Center for Dummies?"*

- Read Chapter 4: *"Isn't the Learning Center for Dummies?"* in the book *Overcoming Life's Trials: Do I Need to Know This for the Final?* Note any insights you want to remember from the book. What questions come to mind that you want to think about some more or bring to the group?

> **"Contrary to popular opinion, prayer is the most tangible and practical thing we can do in the face of a crisis."**
>
> –Gary Mayes, *Now What!*

LOOKING INWARD

Summary of Session 5: In our quest to overcome the challenges and trials of life, we often overlook prayer and run ahead of God or we tend to camp in the prayer closet and lag behind the Lord. James unmistakably relates to us the role prayer plays in passing the test of trials. The gospels record what is typically referred to as the "The Lord's Prayer." It has been suggested that it really is "The Apostles' Prayer" because Jesus is teaching them how to prayer. Comparably James gives us principles on how to pray in the throes of trials, and we shall call it "God's Prayer." Lest we miscommunicate, it is not God praying for us but God who gives us instructions for our prayer to Him. God's Prayer is teaches us to look at our trials from God's viewpoint; to commit our trials to God's character, and to entrust our trials wholeheartedly to God.

"Without a proper understanding of our God, we will not trust Him with our trials. I am reminded of Samuel's interaction with God when the LORD calls his name in 1 Samuel 3:10,

*The LORD came and stood there, calling as at the other times, "Samuel! Samuel!" Then Samuel said, **"Speak, for your servant is listening."***

So often, our prayer is backward: **'Lord, listen for your servant is speaking.'"**

-Overcoming Life's Challenges

Crutches:

Crutches are a source or means of support and assistance. There are instances in life where crutches are needful and some instances where crutches are needless. Some would see prayer as a needful crutch as a means of God's support and assistance. Others would see God and prayer as a needless crutch, because we are strong enough and should be self-sufficient.

Let's think about the following statements. Is each a **crutches needed statement** or a **crutches needless statement**? Put either the word **needed** or **needless** in each blank below to make the statement reflect your opinion.

- Crutches are _____ for a broken leg.

- Crutches are _____ for appendicitis.

- Prayer is a _____ crutch for God's wisdom.

- Prayer is a _____ crutch since *"God helps those who help themselves."*

- *"Contrary to popular opinion, prayer is the most tangible and practical thing we can do in the face of a crisis."*

  -Gary Mayes

  Gary Mayes' statement says prayer is a _____ crutch.

Character Qualities of God for the Test of Trials:

Listed below are the five character qualities of God James gives us to focus on during our times of trials. After reading the five passages, do the following.

1. **Circle:** Put a circle around the one characteristic Jesus wants you to make a conscience effort to keep in mind as you deal with your trial.

2. **Share:** I will share this character quality of God with _____ this week. This is what I will tell him/her about the verse:

3. **Focus:** Write that character quality of God and corresponding verse on a 3x5 card. Put it someplace where you will be reminded of it daily i.e. on your mirror, in your car, at your computer, etc.

→ **God is a *giving* God.**

> For God so loved the world that he gave his one and only Son, that whoever believes in him shall not perish but have eternal life (John 3:16).

→ **God is a *generous* God.**

> So we praise God for the glorious grace he has poured out on us who belong to his dear Son (Ephesians 1:6 NLT).

➜ **God is an *impartial* God.**

> For God does not show favoritism (Romans 2:11; also see - Acts 10:34-35).

➜ **God is a *gracious* God.**

> Let us then approach God's throne of grace with confidence, so that we may receive mercy and find grace to help us in our time of need (Hebrews 4:16).

➜ **God is a *promise-keeping* God.**

> God is not a man, so he does not lie. He is not human, so he does not change his mind. Has he ever spoken and failed to act? Has he ever promised and not carried it through? (Numbers 23:19 NLT).

> **"Though infinitely better able to do without prayer than we are, yet [Christ] prayed much more than we do."**
>
> -Charles Spurgeon

From Doubting to Believing:

But when you ask, you must believe and not doubt, because the one who doubts is like a wave of the sea, blown and tossed by the wind. That person should not expect to receive anything from the Lord. Such a person is double-minded and unstable in all they do.

James 1:6-8

To overcome life's trials, James instructs us to believe God and not doubt God when we pray. From each of the verses below, complete the sentence stating how you can move from being a doubter to a believer.

So God has given both his promise and his oath. These two things are unchangeable because it is impossible for God to lie. Therefore, we who have fled to him for refuge can have great confidence as we hold to the hope that lies before us. This hope is a strong and trustworthy anchor for our souls (Hebrews 6:18-19 NLT).

➜ **From Hebrews 6:18-19, I will believe God by:**

This is the confidence we have in approaching God: that if we ask anything according to his will, he hears us. And if we know that he hears us—whatever we ask—we know that we have what we asked of him (1 John 5:14-15).

➔ **From 1 John 5:14-15, I will believe God by:**

But because my servant Caleb has a different spirit and follows me wholeheartedly, I will bring him into the land [Promised Land] he went to, and his descendants will inherit it (Numbers 14:24).

➔ **From Numbers 14:24, I will believe God by:**

No one can serve two masters. Either you will hate the one and love the other, or you will be devoted to the one and despise the other (Matthew 6:24a).

➔ **From Matthew 6:24a, I will believe God by:**

P.R.A.Y. Model:

Make it a priority to spend some time with God this week. From our session with the group, you were asked to commit to two times to **P.R.A.Y.** Have you kept those appointments with God?

→ Choose one of the options below to take time right now to **P.R.A.Y.**

1. Go back to the group session and use that **P.R.A.Y. Model** to lead you to talk with God about a challenge you are facing.

2. Use the **P.R.A.Y. Model** below to spend time with God as He directs you.

Praise: Praise God for who He is and what He has done.

Repent: Ask God to forgive you for a specific sin(s). Ask God to convict you of sin you need to confess.

Ask: Pray for the needs of three individuals that God places on your heart. Pray for three needs in your life.

Yield: What is an area in your life where you struggle with giving the controls to God? Talk with God about it and pray for a yielded heart.

> "Have you ever watched a bird sleeping on its perch and never falling off? How does it manage to do this? The secret is the tendons of the bird's legs. They are so constructed that when the leg is bent at the knee, the claws contract and grip like a steel trap. The claws refuse to let go until the knees are unbent again. The bended knee gives the bird the ability to hold on to his perch so tightly."
>
> -Rollin S. Burhams

LOOKING FORWARD

Doesn't My Teacher Grade On A Curve?

When we bow the knee of our heart before the Lord in prayer we are doing spiritual battle. In war we must listen to our Commander, that is why it is important to know who God is and spend time talking with him. The constant conflict for us is to move from the rank of doubter to the position of believer in God and His Word. We must continually grapple with "harmonizing our wills with God's." Though the struggle is monumental, it leads us to God's Place in the times of trials. Through the eyes of this world, it does not have much value, but God's Place has out-of-this-world worth. James describes it this way, *"Listen, my dear brothers and sisters: Has not God chosen those who are poor in the eyes of the world to be rich in faith and to inherit the kingdom he promised those who love him?"* (James 2:5).

SESSION 6
DOESN'T MY TEACHER GRADE ON A CURVE?

Let our trials lead us to God's Place

-James 1:9-11

Come Together: *"Two Truths and a Lie"*

(20 minutes) [20/20]

Each person will need to think of two true statements about themselves and make up one lie. They will state all three as though true about themselves. The rest of the group will try to guess which one of the three statements is a lie. Family members, please don't give it away! Once a person has gone, he/she will select the next person to share. Continue until everyone has gone or time is up.

Watch: *"Doesn't My Teacher Grade on a Curve?"*

(20 minutes) [20/40]

> "Because the tests of our trials are not graded on a curve but against the standard of Christ, we must let our trials lead us to God's place. God's place is to focus on our position in Christ and not to be distracted by our earthly position. Not only do trials develop us but they reveal Christ-likeness in each of us, as they escort us to God's place. God's place for us in trials is to hold tightly to our position in Christ and loosely to our position on earth."
>
> *-Overcoming Life's Challenges*

WE PASS THE TEST OF TRIALS BY LETTING OUR TRIALS LEAD US **GOD'S PLACE**.

God's Place for Us in Trials is to Hold _____[1] to Our Position in _____.[2] James 1:9

Believers in humble circumstances ought to take pride in their high position.

James 1:9

1. We hold tightly to our position in Christ but is different than our culture's idea of significance.

   ➤ The believer in humble circumstances depicts a person of _____[3] significance by this world's evaluation or estimation.

   ➤ Jesus uses this same word for _____[4] to describing Himself in Matthew 11:29; **"I am gentle and humble in heart."**

2. We hold tightly to our position in Christ because it is God's idea of significance.

   Praise be to the God and Father of our Lord Jesus Christ, **who has blessed us in the heavenly realms with every spiritual blessing in Christ** (Ephesians 1:3).

   To them God has chosen to make known among the Gentiles the glorious riches of this mystery, **which is Christ in you, the hope of glory** (Colossians 1:27).

   • For God wanted them [believers] to know that the riches and glory of Christ are for you Gentiles, too. And this is the secret: **Christ lives in you. This gives you assurance of sharing his glory** (Colossians 1:27 NLT).

   • But because of his great love for us, God, who is rich in mercy, made us alive with Christ even when we were dead in transgressions—it is by grace you have been saved. **And God raised us up with Christ and seated us with him in the heavenly realms in Christ Jesus** (Ephesians 2:4-6).

   • Since, then, you have been raised with Christ, set your hearts on things above, **where Christ is, seated at the right hand of God**. Set your minds on things above, not on earthly things. For you died, and your life is now hidden with Christ in God (Colossians 3:1-3).

God's Place for Us in Trials is to Hold _____ [5] to Our Position on _____ [6]. James 1:10-11

A. The one who is rich is a believer who has significance in the eyes of this world.

   "But the rich should take pride in their humiliation..."
   James 1:10a [cm. 1 John 2:15-17]

B. Believers have 3 motivating factors to focus on our position in Christ while on earth.

> The temporary nature of life is an incentive to focus on Christ.

"But the rich should take pride in their humiliation—since they will pass away like a wild flower." James 1:10b

> The troubled nature of life illustrates the need to focus on Christ.

"For the sun rises with scorching heat and withers the plant; its blossom falls and its beauty is destroyed." James 1:11a

> The transitory nature of life inevitably brings us to focus on Christ.

"In the same way, the rich will fade away even while they go about their business." James 1:11b

CITZENS OF _____ 7

**But our citizenship is in heaven.
And we eagerly await a Savior from there,
the Lord Jesus Christ**

Philippians 3:20

Group Discussion: *"What Do You Think?"*

(15 minutes)   [15/55]

- Based on what you just learned, how would you explain God's Place to someone?

- What are some ways that we hold tightly to the values of this world?

- What are some ways that we can hold tightly to our place in Christ?

The great mistake made by most of the Lord's people is in hoping to discover in themselves that which is to be found in Christ alone.

-A.W. Pink, Author

Partner Interaction: *"Talk it over with a Friend"*

(10 minutes)   [10/65]

- What value(s) of this world are the hardest for you to let go?

- What can you personally do to focus on your position in Christ?

Take Away: *"My Personal Response"*

God and I:

(10 minutes) [10/75]

→ While you are with a partner:

> ➤ Share your answer: Because of God's Place for me in my trials, how does God want me to think, act, or say differently?

> ➤ Pray for each other: Take a moment to pray for your partner's answer.

Snacks:

(15 minutes) [15/90]

Food for Thot: Honey is the only food that has an eternal shelf life. It will never go bad as long as you live, so don't worry about it spoiling when you go on that long trip. Neither will the Word of God. Check out Psalm 119:103!

How sweet are your words to my taste, sweeter than honey to my mouth!

Psalm 119:103

Answers to Video Session 6: 1-Tightly; 2-Christ; 3-Little; 4-Humble; 5-Loosely; 6-Earth; 7-Heaven

BETWEEN THE SESSIONS – ON YOUR OWN
Doesn't My Teacher Grade On A Curve?

Let our trials lead us to God's Place

-James 1:9-11

LOOKING BACKWARD

- What do you want to remember from video Session 6: *"Doesn't My Teacher Grade on a Curve?"*

- Read Chapter 5: *"Doesn't My Teacher Grade on a Curve?"* in the book *Overcoming Life's Trials: Do I Need to Know This for the Final?* Note any insights you want to remember from the book. What questions come to mind that you want to think about some more or bring to the group?

LOOKING INWARD

Summary of Session 6: We are faced with two contradictory places. One places that gives little significance on eternal values and great value on possessions, pleasures, and position. The other places that gives little significance on the temporary values of this life and places great value on the significance we have in Christ or God's Place. As we pass the test of trials we will hold tightly to our position in Christ, which is God's Place. As we pass the test of trials we will hold loosely to our position on earth, which is our world's value.

"For we who are believers God sees our spiritual position in Christ. Not because of what we have done but because of the incredible and completed work of Jesus Christ. Later, James himself gives us insight into this place that is of little earthly significance but great eternal significance. *"Listen, my dear brothers and sisters:* **Has not God chosen those who are poor in the eyes of the world** *to be rich in faith and to inherit the kingdom he promised those who love him?" (James 2:5).* God's place for the believers in Jesus Christ may be viewed by many as a place of insignificance, but God has chosen to make us rich and give us an inheritance in His place."

-Overcoming Life's Challenges

Who I Am:

*"Do not love the world or the things in the world. If anyone loves the world, the love of the Father is not in him. For all that is in the world—**the desires of the flesh** and **the desires of the eyes** and **pride of life**—is not from the Father but is from the world. And the world is passing away along with its desires, but whoever does the will of God abides forever"* (1 John 2:15-17 ESV).

In the previous verses, the Apostle John tells us what are the values of this world: the desires of the flesh, the desires of the eyes, and the pride of life. These three earthly places create a distraction to keep us from focusing on God's Place. Some of the things in each of these areas are vices and some are not, but they certainly can become temporal things that we hold onto too tightly in lieu of holding onto the eternal. Let's be honest with ourselves and look closely at the grip we have on each of these areas or the grip they have on us.

→ **The Desires of the Flesh: I am one who holds onto PLEASURES.** Some examples of the Desires of the Flesh are: good feelings, overindulging, addictions, etc.

➤ In the place of **PLEASURES**, on a scale of 1 to 10 (1=not really me; 10=really me), I am a _____. The earthly pleasure I hold onto too tightly is:

→ **The Desires of the Eyes: I am one who holds onto POSSESSIONS.** Some examples of the Desires of the Eyes are: stuff I own, things I want, collecting objects, etc.

➤ In the place of **POSSESSIONS**, on a scale of 1 to 10 (1=not really me; 10=really me), I am a _____. The earthly possession I hold onto too tightly is:

→ **The Pride of Life: I am one who holds onto POSITIONS.**
Some examples the Pride of Life are: being the center of attention, being in charge, having or desiring power or authority, etc.

➢ In the place of **POSITIONS**, on a scale of 1 to 10 (1=not really me; 10=really me), I am a _____. The earthly position I hold onto too tightly is:

> **"James' point, then, is that believers must look beyond the world's evaluation to understand who they are and look at God's view of them."**
>
> -Douglas Moo, Commentator

Who I Am In Christ:

At the moment of our salvation we are located in Christ, God's Place. Theologian Lewis Sperry Chafer[F] denotes thirty-three gifts given to us in Christ the instant we experience saving faith. These gifts describe who we are in Christ. Below are a few of them. Regardless of what anyone may say or think about you, this is an accurate description of who you are in Christ, God's Place. Put your name on the line beside each description. Read each one five times slowly, thoughtfully, and deliberately. Let the reality of who you are in Christ-God's Place become absorbed into the fiber of your being.

[F] "Things Accomplished at Salvation"; Dr. Lewis Chafer, <u>Chafer Systematic Theology</u>: 8 volumes (Dallas: Dallas Seminary Press, 1983), volume 3.

_____ is a child of God.

See how very much our Father loves us, for he calls us his children, and that is what we are! (1 John 3:1a NLT).

_____ is acceptable to God through Jesus Christ.

Accept one another, then, just as Christ accepted you, in order to bring praise to God (Romans 15:7).

_____ is justified.

[Justified means I am declared and treated as not guilty because of Jesus' work.]

Therefore, since we have been justified by faith, we have peace with God through our Lord Jesus Christ (Romans 5:1 ESV).

_____ is forgiven all sins.

When you were dead in your sins and in the uncircumcision of your flesh, God made you alive with Christ. He forgave us all our sins... (Colossians 2:13).

_____ is redeemed.

[Redeemed means I am purchased by the blood of Jesus Christ out of the slave market of sin and now free in Christ.]

In him [Jesus Christ] we have redemption through his blood, the forgiveness of our trespasses, according to the riches of his grace that he lavished on us in all wisdom and insight (Ephesians 1:7-8 NET).

_____ is reconciled.

[Reconciled means I am now a friend of God. Reconciliation means I was God's enemy, but in Christ I am now a friend of God.]

For if while we were enemies we were reconciled to God through the death of his Son, how much more, since we have been reconciled, will we be saved by his life? (Romans 5:10 NET).

→ Which one of the passages above makes you say, "Wow!" Write below what that means to you as you encounter the challenges of life.

→ From this sample of the 33 gifts given to us in Christ, God's Place, what are three truths about being in Christ you had not thought of before?

1.

2.

3.

Hold'n Tight and Hang'n Loose:

LOOSELY: LET IT GO - From "Who I Am" what is **one earthly thing** you need to hold more loosely? How will you do it?

TIGHTLY: HOLD ONTO IT - From "Who I Am In Christ" what are **two heavenly truths** do you need to hold onto more tightly? How will you do it?

Pass It On:

→ Which of the "Who I Am In Christ" passages best helps you understand **God's Place** for you?

→ **Choose** someone to share this passage with. Send an email, write a letter, call, or tell them in person. Who will you tell? When will you tell him/her?

→ **Memorize**: Philippians 3:20, *"But our citizenship is in heaven. And we eagerly await a Savior from there, the Lord Jesus Christ."*

Ask a friend to keep you accountable to memorize the verse.
Better yet, have a friend memorize it with you!

LOOKING FORWARD

I'm Being Recognized at the Awards' Ceremony!?

Wow, what an incomprehensible position we have in Christ! When we focus on God's Place for us then we are able to look at trials as they are: temporal and earthly. We are able to hold more tightly to the heavenly, eternal things. This is where we join the Apostle Paul when he said, *"We live by faith, not by sight"* (2 Corinthians 5:7). This great position we have in Christ will one day become a reality. It is that future reality James addresses as he gives us God's Promise in the midst of our trials.

SESSION 7
I'M BEING RECOGNIZED AT THE AWARDS' CEREMONY!?

Remember Our Trials Have God's Promise

-James 1:12

Come Together: *"And the Award Goes to..."*

(20 minutes)   [20/20]

Through the time you have spent together, undoubtedly you have learned some interesting things about each member of your group. Give an award to each individual in your group. For example, the person who is always late to the group could win the: "Most likely to be late to his/her own funeral award." You can use the sample phrase below, or you may want to come up with your own "Overcoming Life's Challenges Awards." Be creative, be sensitive not to hurt anyone, but **HAVE FUN!!**

→ _____ is most likely to

Accept one another, then, just as Christ accepted you, in order to bring praise to God.
                                        Romans 15:7

Snacks:

(15 minutes) [15/35]

Food for Thot: The popsicle was "invented" by an eleven-year-old. Most eleven-year-olds invent "mud pies." What did you invent when you were eleven?

→ Feel free to grab some more snacks and a drink and gather around to watch the Video.

Watch: *"I'm Being Recognized at the Awards' Ceremony!?"*

(20 minutes) [20/55]

"Just as we find in the school setting, God in His Word gives us notification about the rewards we may receive. Even more than a school or a person, God keeps His promises. Each believer in Jesus Christ will stand at the judgment seat of Christ. As we stand before the Lord Jesus, we may receive a crown we didn't expect. We may receive a crown with humble jubilation. But rest assured, Jesus Christ will keep His promise regarding the test of trials."

-Overcoming Life's Challenges

WE PASS THE TEST OF TRIALS BY

REMEMBERING OUR TRIALS HAVE

GOD'S PROMISE.

→ At the first three checkpoints, we climb God's observation tower to view our trials from His vantage point: **God's Power, God's Perspective, and God's Purpose.**

→ At the second three checkpoints, we climb our observation tower to view out trials from our vantage point: **God's Prayer, God's Place, and God's Promise.**

God's Promise is a _____,[1] When We _____[2] Under Our Trials. James 1:12a

Blessed is the one who perseveres under trial because, having stood the test, that person will receive the crown of life that the Lord has promised to those who love him.
James 1:12

1. When we endure trials, God declares us happy.

   ➢ **Blessed** means to be pronounced or declared _____.[3]

2. When we endure trials, God develops our faith.

> ➤ **Perseverance** means to remain under trying circumstances for a long time.

> ➤ James 1:12a focuses on the last part of our definition: "A trial is a test God uses to prove the genuineness of our faith and **to develop our maturity in Jesus Christ.**"

God's Promise is a _____,[4] When We _____[5] Our Faith is Genuine through our Trials. James 1:12b

Blessed is the one who perseveres under trial because, having stood the test, that person will receive the crown of life that the Lord has promised to those who love him. James 1:12

1. God's reward is given to those whose faith is genuine, so prove it now!

"...**because**, having stood the test..." James 1:12

> ➤ James 1:12b focuses on the first part of our definition: "A trial is a test God uses **to prove the genuineness of our faith** and to develop our maturity in Jesus Christ."

2. God's reward is given in the future, so persevere now!

   "...**because** that person will receive the crown of life..."
   James 1:12

   His master replied, "Well done, good and faithful servant! You have been faithful with a few things; I will put you in charge of many things. Come and share your master's happiness!" (Matthew 25:21).

3. God's reward is given to those who love God, so obey Him now!

   "...**because** that the Lord has promised to those who love him. James 1:12

   If you love me, keep my commands (John 14:15).

   In fact, this is love for God: to keep his commands. And his commands are not burdensome... (1 John 5:3).

"Come to me, all you who are weary and burdened, and I will give you rest. Take my yoke upon you and learn from me, for I am gentle and humble in heart, and you will find rest for your souls. For my yoke is easy and my burden is light."

-Jesus (Matthew 11:28-30)

"Jesus, _____ [6] love you!"

"They [trials] are not problems to avoid, crises to endure, tests to pass; they are expressions of our love for our Savior Jesus Christ. When yielded to Him we can find joy in the trial and strength to obey. Right now, each of us is staring into the eyes of a trial, a testing of our faith. We know what God wants us to do about it, so without further delay obey. Take this precious opportunity to tell Jesus, 'I love you!'"

-Overcoming Life's Challenges

Group Discussion: *"What Do You Think?"*

(20 minutes)   [20/75]

- James 1:12 tells us, *"Blessed is the one who perseveres under trial because, having stood the test, that person will receive the crown of life that the Lord has promised to those who love him."* What does the word **"Blessed"** mean? How does this understanding change your outlook on trials?

- The crown of life is given to those who stand the test of trials and is God's Promise to those who love Jesus. How do we love Jesus (see John 14:15)?

- The Apostle John also tells us in 1 John 5:3 that God's commands are not a burden. When do His commands become a burden? How do we prevent God's commands from becoming burdensome?

- ***"A trial is a test God uses to prove the genuineness of our faith and to develop our maturity in Jesus Christ."*** What does James 1:12 add to give us a fuller understanding of our definition of trials?

Take Away: *"My Personal Response"*

(5 minutes)   [5/80]

➔ Lord, based on this session, I believe You want me to:

> **The Lord's commands are rarely accompanied with reasons but they are always accompanied with promises, either expressed or understood.**
>
> -A.W. Pink, Author

God and I:

(10 minutes)   [10/90]

In the time you have left, take prayer requests. Write them here and pray for the request at least 3 times this week.

Answers to Video Session 7: 1-Blessing; 2-Persevere; 3-Happy; 4-Reward; 5-Prove; 6-I

BETWEEN THE SESSIONS – ON YOUR OWN
I'm Being Recognized at the Awards' Ceremony!?
Remember Our Trials Have God's Promise
-James 1:12

LOOKING BACKWARD

- What do you want to remember from video Session 7: *"I'm Being Recognized at the Awards' Ceremony!?"*

- Read chapter 6: *"I'm Getting Recognized at the Awards' Ceremony!?"* in the book *Overcoming Life's Trials: Do I Need to Know This for the Final?* Note any insights you want to remember from the book. What questions come to mind that you want to think about some more or bring to the group?

LOOKING INWARD

Summary of Session 7: In chapter 1 verse 12, James gives us the last principle to guide us on how to pass the tests of trials. As we seek to overcome life's challenges, we are to keep in mind God's Promise. God's Promise in trials reveals two principles for us: 1) God's promise is a blessing, when we persevere under our trials; 2) God's promise is a reward, when we prove our faith is genuine through our trials.

"James has methodically been put together a puzzle for us, and now every piece is tightly interlocking to bring the picture of the first twelve verses together. These pieces of God's power, perspective, purpose, prayer, place, and promise now form a message of love to Jesus Christ. James connects these pieces in such a way as to strengthen and build our love for Jesus, so our lives will shout, 'Jesus, I love You!'"

-Overcoming Life's Challenges

In Your Trophy Case:

List three **accomplishments**, **recognitions,** or **awards** you are thankful to have received. Beside each one, write a reason why you are proud of that accomplishment, recognition, or award. This is not being prideful. Follow the Apostle Paul's instructions for self-evaluation and reflection: *"Don't think you are better than you really are. Be honest in your evaluation of yourselves"* (Romans 12:3 NLT).

1.

2.

3.

Stand on God's Promise:

James 1:12 reveals two principles about God's Promise in our trials. Take a look at the two principles, and see how you are doing in the test of trials.

God's Promise is a blessing, when we persevere under out trials.

"Blessed is the one who perseveres under trial..."
James 1:12a

→ What does it mean to be *"Blessed?"*
- ❑ God declares or pronounces us happy.
- ❑ God gives us everything we want.
- ❑ God turns what we do into a success.

→ Who is *"Blessed?"*
- ❑ The person who is doing all the things a Christian should do.
- ❑ The person who is hanging in there under a trial.
- ❑ The person who is giving a lot of money to the church.

→ When are we *"declared happy?"*
- ❑ When we die.
- ❑ When we are told to have a "Blessed Day."
- ❑ When we persevere under trials.

➜ Why are we *"declared happy?"*

❑ Because we withstood the trials of life until we developed the maturity of Christ.

❑ Because we were able to avoid the challenges of life until we didn't have any more.

❑ Because we wanted to receive the Crown of Life.

God's Promise is a reward, when we prove our faith is genuine through our trials.

"Because having stood the test, that person will receive the crown of life that the Lord has promised to those who love him."
James 1:12b

➜ Who will receive the *"Crown of Life?"*

❑ The person who stands the test.

❑ The person who wants it.

❑ The person who never fails a test of trials.

➜ What do we prove when we stand the test of trials?

❑ That we have the heart of a human.

❑ That we have genuine faith.

❑ That we have achieved a sinless life.

➜ When will we receive the *"Crown of Life?"*

❑ Before our faith is tested.

❑ During the testing of our faith.

❑ After we have withstood the testing of our faith.

➜ Why will we receive the *"Crown of Life?"*

❑ Because God has promised it to those who demonstrate their faith is genuine.

❑ Because we have earned it due to all the good things we have done.

❑ Because that's just the kind of God we have.

Keep Your Focus On God's Future:

Although English grammar may not be our favorite subject, it does help us to live out the principle of remembering our trials have God's Promise. In English grammar the present tense is currently happening, "**I am** experiencing the tests of trials." The future tense is yet to happen, "**I will** receive the crown of life." What we do in this present life will impact our future life.

> **"God is a sure paymaster, though He does not always pay at the end of every week."**
> -Charles Spurgeon

→ In the trial you are facing right now, how can you prove your faith is genuine?

→ In the trial you are facing right now, how can you persevere?

→ In the trial you are facing right now, how can you obey God?

In all this you greatly rejoice, though now for a little while you may have had to suffer grief in all kinds of trials. These have come so that the proven genuineness of your faith—of greater worth than gold, which perishes even though refined by fire—may result in praise, glory and honor when Jesus Christ is revealed.

1 Peter 1:6-7

"Jesus, I Love You!"

→ In John 14:15 Jesus says that if **we obey His commands**, we let Jesus know we love Him. What commands do you need to obey right now to express your love to Jesus?

→ In Matthew 11:28-30 Jesus gives us **His words of comfort** to come to Him with our burdens, and He will give us rest. What burden do you need to give Jesus in exchange for His comfort and rest?

→ In 1 John 5:3 John tells us **Jesus' commands are not a burden**. Which commands of Jesus have become a burden to you? What do you need to do to turn those burdensome commands into expressions of love for the Savior?

LOOKING FORWARD

The Commencement Address

As we look forward to commencement, which is really a new beginning, let us review this lesson on God's Promise in the test of trials. We store our treasures in heaven, not in earthly temporal treasures. We take our stand on God's Promise, not on our unreliable selves. We keep our focus on God's future, not on our present circumstances. We show our love for Jesus with joyful obedience, not by our burdened efforts. Now, let us review the study guide containing all the principles on "How to pass the test of trials," and remember the question is not "Do I need to know this for the final?" The question is "Have I learned my lessons of faith to the point where I consistently exhibit real faith and constantly grow in Christ-likeness?" Let us listen intently to the commencement address and be mindful of Jesus' words to us: *"Do not store up for yourselves treasures on earth, where moths and vermin destroy, and where thieves break in and steal. But store up for yourselves treasures in heaven, where moths and vermin do not destroy, and where thieves do not break in and steal. For where your treasure is, there your heart will be also"* (Matthew 6:19-21).

SESSION 8
THE COMMENCEMENT ADDRESS

Partner Interaction: *"Talk it over with a Friend"*

(20 minutes)   [20/20]

- What kinds of challenges are you experiencing right now?

  ❑ Mental

  ❑ Emotional

  ❑ Physical

  ❑ Relational

  ❑ Spiritual

  ❑ Other

> **"Better the storm with Christ than smooth waters without Him."**
>
> - Unknown

- Of the six principles we have examined, which one do you need right now to address the main challenge you noted above? Explain why.

- ❏ We pass the test of trials by yielding our trials to God's Power.
- ❏ We pass the test of trials by seeing our trials from God's Perspective.
- ❏ We pass the test of trials by understanding our trials accomplish God's Purpose.
- ❏ We pass the test of trials by allowing our trials to teach us God's Prayer.
- ❏ We pass the test of trials by letting our trials lead us to God's Place.
- ❏ We pass the test of trials by remembering our trials have God's Promise.

- Share this with your partner or answer on your own: Lord, based on the above, I believe You want me to:

Watch: *"The Commencement Address"*

(20 minutes)   [20/40]

"Commencement means a point at which something begins."

-*Overcoming Life's Challenges*

THE COMMENCEMENT ADDRESS:
A BEGINNING

The Commencement Address of a Phrase

➔ **The Phrase: "Mtafute Mungu Kwanza!"**

S_____[1] Jesus is the pursuit of your life.

G_____[2] Jesus is the passion of your life.

F_____[3] Jesus is the priority of your life.

But seek first his kingdom and his righteousness, and all these things will be given to you as well.

Matthew 6:33

The Commencement Address of a Principle

➔ **The Principle: "_____[4] what it says!"**

Therefore everyone who hears these words of mine and puts them into practice is like a wise man who built his house on the rock (Matthew 7:24).

The Commencement Address of a Poem

→ **The Poem: "The _____ [5] Weaver"**

My life is but a weaving,

Between my God and me.

I do not choose the colours,

He works so steadily.

Oft' times He weaveth sorrow,

And I in foolish pride,

Forget He sees the upper,

And I the underside.

Not 'til the loom is silent,

And the shuttles cease to fly,

Will God unroll the canvas,

And reveal the reason why.

The dark threads are as needful,

In the Weaver's skillful hand.

As the threads of gold and silver,

In the pattern He has planned. [G]

Yet you, LORD, are our Father. We are the clay, you are the potter; we are all the work of your hand.

Isaiah 64:8

[G] "The Divine Weaver" (The Tapestry Poem) quoted by Corrie ten Boom. Often is attributed to an unknown author but the author may be Grant Colfax Tuller.

The Commencement Address of Power

→ **The Power: "We Are _____[6] Than Conquerors!"**

"More than conquerors" means we have abundantly more than we need to be victorious because of Jesus' love for us.

No, in all these things we are more than conquerors through him who loved us.

Romans 8:37

The Commencement Address for us is to begin *Overcoming Life's Challenges* because we have more than we need to conquer them through the love of Jesus Christ.

Group Discussion: *"What Do You Think?"*

(20 minutes) [20/60]

- How does Corrie ten Boom's life model the principles of passing the test of trials?

- How could you use the poem, *"The Divine Weaver,"* to explain to a friend the way God uses trials in our lives?

- Read Romans 8:31-39. Why are Paul's words a great "Commencement Address" as we begin Overcoming Life's Challenges?

- Many times graduating classes have a motto or even a verse. How is Romans 8:37 a fitting motto for our class as we begin Overcoming Life's Challenges?

Eat: *"Everyone bring a dish and eat together"*

(30 minutes)   [30/90]

> **"We look at life from the back side of the tapestry. And most of the time, what we see is loose threads, tangled knots and the like. But occasionally, God's light shines through the tapestry, and we get a glimpse of the larger design with God weaving together the darks and lights of existence."**
>
> -John Piper, Author

Food for Thot: If you can get your hands on a really ripe cranberry, try bouncing it like a bouncy ball. Word on the street is they're supposed to bounce sky high.

Answers to Video Session 8: 1-Seek; 2-God; 3-First; 4-Do; 5-Divine; 6-More

AFTER THE SESSIONS– ON YOUR OWN

The Commencement Address

Summary

LOOKING BACKWARD

- What do you want to remember from video Session 8: *"The Commencement Address.?"*

- Read the Summary: *"The Commencement Address"* in the book *Overcoming Life's Trials: Do I Need to Know This for the Final?* Note any insights you want to remember from the book.

LOOKING INWARD

Summary of Session 8: When we come to the end of our schooling, we usually attend a Commencement Service where a guest speaker is invited to give the Commencement Address. Because commencement means "a point at which something begins," generally, the commencement address endeavors to motivate the graduates as they begin a new phase in their lives. Let us look inward and begin to Overcome Life's Challenges by living by the principles James taught us.

"James' commencement address would tell us: 'Don't just listen to these six principles and cram them in your heads to know for the test of trials. Learn them until they are a part of who you are, continuing to do them until your faith is your own and your lives take on the qualities of Jesus Christ."

-Overcoming Life's Challenges

Overcoming Life's Challenges:

→ What kinds of challenges are you experiencing right now?

❑ Mental

❑ Emotional

❑ Physical

❑ Relational

❑ Spiritual

❑ Other

Putting All the Pieces Together:

Below are listed the six principles we learned in the school of hard knocks. This is the time of new beginnings to live them out in our everyday challenges. Write out each principle in your own words.

Principle #1: We pass the test of trials by yielding our trials to God's Power.

Principle #2: We pass the test of trials by seeing our trials from God's Perspective.

Principle #3: We pass the test of trials by understanding our trials accomplish God's Purpose.

Principle #4: We pass the test of trials by allowing our trials to teach us God's Prayer.

Principle #5: We pass the test of trials by letting our trials lead us to God's Place.

Principle #6: We pass the test of trials by remembering our trials have God's Promise.

➔ Which one of the principles does Jesus wants you to make a conscious effort to work on over this next month?

➔ How does Jesus wants you to pray about that principle each day this week? Check no more than two. Then intentionally focus your prayers on those two.

❑ To see it from God's viewpoint

❑ To pray with a sense of urgency

❑ To trust this character quality of God:

_____

❑ To listen to God

❑ To harmonize my will His

❑ To not be a doubter

❑ To believe God will meet with me

❑ Other:

❑ Other:

If you falter in a time of trouble, how small is your strength!
Proverbs 24:10

➔ Which member of your family and/or friends is struggle with a trial? Select one of the principles you can to encourage him/her this week.

> Who is that individual(s)?

> What principle will you share with him/her?

> When will you plan on sharing the principle?

> How will you communicate this principle in a way that encourages your friend and/or family member?

> Why is this principle important to you? Why is it important to share with him/her?

LOOKING FORWARD

More Than Conquerors

As noted, commencement means a point at which something begins, not the end. If it is the end of anything, it is the end of the way we used to deal with life's challenges. Now we are launching into God's way of overcoming life's challenges. We begin this new journey by connecting to **God's Power** as we surrendering ourselves to Him. We look at challenges through God's lens, in order to have **God's Perspective**. When we grasp better what God is doing through our challenges, we allow **God's Purpose** to be accomplished in us. Each challenge drives us to harmonize our will to His as we learn how to pray **God's Prayer** in the midst of trials. We have confidence in Christ because we are in **God's Place** during the onslaught of trouble. We begin to look forward to **God's Promise** to those who withstand the test and love the Lord Jesus Christ.

As we come to the end of our time together, begin by looking forward to being *"More than a conqueror through the love of Christ"* to Overcome Life's Challenges.

Romans 8:31-39

→ To you what words and/or phrases that leap off the page? Highlight or mark them.

What, then, shall we say in response to these things? If God is for us, who can be against us? He who did not spare his own Son, but gave him up for us all—how will he not also, along with him, graciously give us all things? Who will bring any charge against those whom God has chosen? It is God who justifies. Who then is the one who condemns? No one. Christ Jesus who died—more than that, who was raised to life—is at the right hand of God and is also interceding for us. Who shall separate us from the love of Christ? Shall trouble or hardship or persecution or famine or nakedness or danger or sword? As it is written: "For your sake we face death all day long; we are considered as sheep to be slaughtered." **No, in all these things we are more than conquerors through him who loved us.** For I am convinced that neither death nor life, neither angels nor demons, neither the present nor the future, nor any powers, neither height nor depth, nor anything else in all creation, will be able to separate us from the love of God that is in Christ Jesus our Lord.

→ We are told that *"we are more than conquerors through him who loved us."* "More than conquerors" means we have abundantly more than we need to be victorious because of Jesus' love for us. When facing life's challenges, what can you do to live as God sees you: **"a super abundant victor in Christ?"**

- ❑ In thought:
- ❑ In attitude:
- ❑ In action:
- ❑ In words:

→ What is Jesus saying to you from Romans 8:31-39? Imagine Jesus is writing a note to you in your graduation card. Write below that note from Jesus to you, encouraging you as you commence in following Him to Overcome Life's Challenges.

Dear:

I love you,

Jesus

NOTES

NOTES

FACILITATOR'S INFO

TIPS:

1. Facilitators will want to be familiar with the "How to use the Participant's Guide" section.

2. Facilitators are encouraged to tailor the sessions to best fit their group's needs and their facilitating experience. Some facilitators are new and need more guidance. Some facilitators are more seasoned in leading a group and know how they want their groups to go. The times and components are a suggested guideline, but facilitators are encouraged to adapt to their specific group and the facilitator's style.

3. Facilitators need to have a general game plan for each session. This will guide the facilitator in keeping the group moving and when to spend more time on a particular component. This will change as you get more familiar with your group.

4. Facilitators should work to encourage each group member to participate at their level of comfort. You can include quieter members by asking them to read verses, questions, or respond to general questions.

5. Facilitators also need to be alert to the individual(s) who tend to do all the talking and dominate the discussion. Try to include others as recommended above; suggest that several people respond to the question or someone who has not said much yet.

6. Facilitators need to be aware of allowing time for individuals to respond to the Holy Spirit's promptings. Plan time for application. Don't be afraid of silence.

7. Facilitators, be mindful that some sessions have "Snacks" right after Watching the Video. This is to allow individuals to stretch, take a short break, and grab a snack for the Group Discussion. Keep an eye on your time here.

COME TOGETHER ACTIVITIES:

Each of the Come Together Activities is designed to build community within your group. Some of them tie directly into the session. Please take time to read each activity and its intended purpose. Feel free to adapt, change, or not use the prescribed "Come Together Activity." Every group is different in what they like and comfort level. Try to stretch your group. Whatever you choose to do, please allow time for group building at each of your sessions. Below is a further explanation of the Come Together Activity from each session.

Session #1: *"Who's My Neighbor?"*

This can be a great way to break the ice and begin to get to know each other. Even if the group knows each other well, you will still discover something you did not know.

Session #2: *"Highs and Lows"*

This can help individuals to go a little deeper and begin to share about their life's challenges. Be alert to the highs and celebrate them. Be alert to the lows to minister and/or pray for individuals.

Session #3: *"The Eye Clinic"*

The may seem a little goofy but it ties in with an illustration from the lesson on perspective in trials. It can also help identify where individuals are in overcoming the challenges of life.

Session #4: *"What is the Purpose of this Object?"*
Again, this may seem odd, but it ties in with the lesson on purpose in trials. If your group is up for it, here is a fun twist. Get an old blanket and cut a slit in the middle. Place 2 tables next to each other. Before the group arrives have an individual get between the tables with his/her head out the slit in the blanket. Cover the head along with the other objects. When the volunteers lift the towel/blanket to identify the object, have the person yell. Make sure you choose the right volunteers, and it can be a lot of fun! Be sure you have a prize for the "winners."

Session #5: P.R.A.Y.
Follow the instructions in session #5 and give the P.R.A.Y. model a try. This is a tremendous model to use to lead your group in praying together. It may be a little out of your group's comfort zones, but as a facilitator be familiar with the model and go for it. Prayer brings your group together, deepens the relationships, and provides opportunity to meet with Jesus.

Session #6: *"Two Truths and a Lie"*
By this time your group should be getting to know one another, so let's give them a new challenge. Some may have difficulty with this "Come Together Activity" but remind the group it's for fun and to continue to build the group. You will find out some interesting things about your group.

Session #7: *"And the Award Goes To..."*
This one might be a bit more difficult but it ties in with the session. You may want to have a few "Awards" in mind to get the ball rolling, or you may to want come with awards for everyone. A word of caution: have fun with it but be careful not to give "awards" that might be construed by the individual as put downs or hurtful.

Session #8: *Eat*
Make sure you allow plenty of time for your group to come together around a meal. Take time the week before to discuss and organize the meal.

OPTIONS:

1. **Service Project Night:** Your group may want to set aside a night to do a service project. The group may want to take a little time each week to plan and work towards a way your group can reach out

2. **Prayer Night:** Each session has a small prayer time built in, and session number five has a longer time built in; however, your group may want to set aside their whole time together to send in prayer.

3. **Eat Together Night:** Eating together is a great way to build community and relationships within your group. Each session has a snack time built in, and session number eight has a more extended time for each person to bring some food in order to have a meal together. Your group may want to get together on another night to go out to eat or have everyone bring food to share a special meal together.

4. **Social Night:** Each session has the "Come Together Activity" built in; however, your group may want to plan a night for a social activity. It could be a game night, a movie night, going to a park, or going to some kind of event. This may or may not include families of your group. This can be a really good way for individuals to feel more connected and comfortable in sharing their challenges when the group meets.

ACKNOWLEDGEMENTS

Thanks to....

Sarah Buchan for help in capturing the concept for the cover and into a visual reality. www.sarahbuchanphotography.com

Tara Dunn for her assistance on the interior formatting.

Dr. Jerrod Fellhauer for his insight on test anxiety and website information.

Mike Grubbs for saying, "If God wants you to write, sit down and write!"

Dave Kennedy for assistance in writing the introduction for the "When Will I Ever Use This in Real Life?" chapter by sharing his insight from over 40 years of teaching.

Dr. Kris Schuler for her eyes of editing, and the encouragement that came with her reviews.

Suzanne Williams, my sister, for volunteering to bring another set of eyes to the manuscript and for her invaluable recommendations.

Noah for letting me bounce ideas off him and for putting together the website.

Josiah for asking, "Dad, why don't you write?"

Micah for guiding my thoughts as we talked about the introduction to the question: "If you were on trial for being a Christian, would there be enough evidence for a jury to convict you?"

Mom and Dad for being the first to read my very, very rough family manuscript, and continually believing in me.

Jenny Wildman for asking when my next book is coming out.

Daisy for training me to give her a treat every time I sat down at the computer.

ABOUT THE AUTHOR

Steve Baird and his wife Lisa have been married for thirty years. They have two college age sons and one high school age son. During those thirty years they have ministered together, with Steve serving as a Youth Pastor, a Senior Pastor, College Instructor, College Administrator, and a minister in a local church. Steve earned a Bachelor's of Arts Degree in Theology and a Master's of Arts Degree in biblical languages.

Steve Baird is a creative and gifted communicator committed to speaking God's unchanging Word to an ever-changing world. God has graciously given him opportunities to pursue his passion of teaching God's Word in a variety of settings. Steve has lead workshops at two National Youth Conventions, been the featured speaker at camps, a guest instructor and commencement speaker at the Nassau Theological College in Tanzania, a regular guest speaker for Campus Crusade, and a co-chaplain for the University of Nebraska at Kearney football team.

Steve Baird is the founder of E710 Ministries, a speaking and writing ministry. The ministry is based on the description of Ezra as told to us in Ezra 7:10 (ESV), *"For Ezra had set his heart to study the Law of the LORD, and to do it and to teach his statutes and rules in Israel."* E710 Ministries exists to assist individuals in encountering the written and living Christ, resulting in life change. E710 Ministries' mission is to dig into the depths of God's Word, to present Jesus Christ in an understandable way, and to allow the Spirit to change lives.

Check out E710 Ministries: www.e710ministries.com

While you're there, Steve invites you make a comment on this book, discover more about his writings, and inquire about having him speak at your next event.

HOPE TO HEAR FROM YOU!!

OVERCOMING LIFE'S CHALLENGES:
"Do I Need to Know This for the Final?"

At this very moment, each of us finds ourselves going into, in the middle of, or coming out of one of life's challenges. Whether the challenge is mental, emotional, relational, physical or spiritual, we experience the testing of our faith daily. God's desire for us is to not merely pass the test but to demonstrate our faith is genuine and develop the character of Jesus Christ. As we attend the school of hard knocks together, lets us learn principles from James that will enable us to Overcome Life's Challenges!

Overcoming Life's Challenges: Do I Need to Know This for the Final? is the book that provides the foundation and background for the eight session *Overcoming Life's Challenges Participant's Guide* and DVD.

"I have greatly enjoyed working through Steve Baird's "Overcoming Life's Challenges" with my men's small group. We found the book to be insightful and helpful in guiding our examination of the scriptural basis for the trials in our lives. I heartily recommend this book both for personal study and for small group use."
Kelly Walter| Founding Pastor
Rock Brook Church

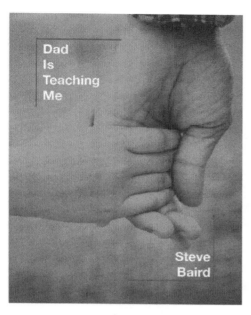

DAD IS
TEACHING ME
IS FOR YOU!!

Whether you are a man, a woman, a boy, or a girl, this booklet is a gift to YOU!! From the beginning to the end, you will unwrap timeless principles revealing the heart of our *Heavenly Father*. In His unmeasurable wisdom, our Heavenly Father has designed *Earthly Fathers* to be a visible representation of Him and to be instrumental in writing their children's stories. Sprinkled throughout this gift, you find children sharing their stories of what their *Earthly Fathers* taught them. This booklet guides *Earthly Fathers* to become men of God and provides them with useful steps to instruct their children in the Lord. As you remove the gift wrapping from each lesson in *Dad Is Teaching Me,* learn from an *Earthly Father* whose life says, *"My son, give me your heart, and let your eyes keep to my ways"* (Proverb 23:26).

"WOW! That is an incredible devotional. I was ministered to while reading it. You have picked out some key topics and written so well. Hats off to you and May God cause Dads to be better followers and imitators of Christ."   -Clay, father of 3 sons

COMING SOON

NAVIGATING LIFE'S MAZE
Following Abraham's Steps to the Will of God

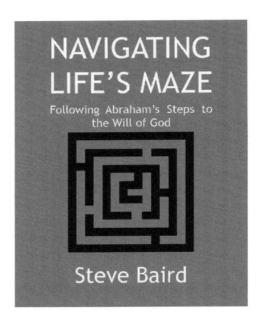

(Not final cover)

We hope to finally turn that corner in life which will be a clear path to God's will for us. In reality, we turn that corner only to find a wall, and another turn. Life can be is like a maze, so how do we navigate it? At times we feel God is hiding His will, but He wants us to know and do His will more than we do. Let's travel back to a time when God navigated Abraham through the maze of his life. *"Leave your country, your people and your father's household and go to the land I will show you"* (Genesis 12:1). As we follow Abraham's footsteps, we discover timeless principles that God uses to guide each of us through Life's Maze!

49153714R00084

Made in the USA
Middletown, DE
18 June 2019